MW00657639

Ranching Women in Southern Alberta

THE WEST SERIES
Aritha van Herk, Series Editor
ISSN 1922-6519 (Print) ISSN 1925-587X (Online)

This series focuses on creative nonfiction that explores our sense of place in the West – how we define ourselves as Westerners and what impact we have on the world around us. Essays, biographies, memoirs, and insights into Western Canadian life and experience are highlighted.

No. 1 Looking Back: Canadian Women's Prairie Memoirs and Intersections of Culture, History, and Identity **S. Leigh Matthews**

No. 2 Catch the Gleam: Mount Royal, From College to University, 1910–2009 **Donald N. Baker**

No. 3 Always an Adventure: An Autobiography **Hugh A. Dempsey**

No. 4 Promoters, Planters, and Pioneers: The Course and Context of Belgian Settlement in Western Canada **Cornelius J. Jaenen**

No. 5 Happyland: A History of the "Dirty Thirties" in Saskatchewan, 1914–1937 **Curtis R. McManus**

No. 6 My Name Is Lola **Lola Rozsa, as told to and written by Susie Sparks**

No. 7 The Cowboy Legend: Owen Wister's Virginian and the Canadian-American Frontier **John Jennings**

No. 8 Sharon Pollock: First Woman of Canadian Theatre **Edited by Donna Coates**

No. 9 Finding Directions West: Readings That Locate and Dislocate Western Canada's Past **Edited by George Colpitts and Heather Devine**

No. 10 Writing Alberta: Building on a Literary Identity **Edited by George Melnyk and Donna Coates**

No. 11 Ranching Women in Southern Alberta **Rachel Herbert**

UNIVERSITY OF CALGARY
Press

RANCHING WOMEN

IN SOUTHERN ALBERTA

Rachel Herbert

RACHEL HERBERT

The West Series
ISSN 1922-6519 (Print) ISSN 1925-587X (Online)

University of Calgary Press
2500 University Drive NW
Calgary, Alberta
Canada T2N 1N4
press.ucalgary.ca

LIBRARY AND ARCHIVES CANADA CATALOGUING IN PUBLICATION

Herbert, Rachel, 1980-, author
Ranching women in southern Alberta / Rachel Herbert.
(The West series, ISSN 1922-6519 ; no. 11)
Includes bibliographical references and index.
Issued in print and electronic formats.
ISBN 978-1-55238-911-9 (softcover).—ISBN 978-1-55238-912-6 (Open Access PDF).—ISBN 978-1-55238-913-3 (PDF). —ISBN 978-1-55238-914-0 (EPUB).—ISBN 978-1-55238-915-7 (Kindle)

1. Women ranchers—Alberta—History—19th century. 2. Women ranchers—Alberta—History—20th century. 3. Ranch life—Alberta—History—19th century. 4. Ranch life—Alberta—History—20th century. 5. Ranches—Alberta—History—19th century. 6. Ranches—Alberta—History—20th century. I. Title. II. Series: West series (Calgary, Alta.) ; 11

FC3670.R3H47 2017   636'.010820971234   C2017-904684-5
C2017-904685-3

The University of Calgary Press acknowledges the support of the Government of Alberta through the Alberta Media Fund for our publications. We acknowledge the financial support of the Government of Canada. We acknowledge the financial support of the Canada Council for the Arts for our publishing program.

This book has been published with the help of a grant from the Alberta Historical Resources Foundation, made possible by the Alberta Lottery Fund.

Alberta Government   Canada   Canada Council for the Arts   Conseil des Arts du Canada   Alberta Historical Resources Foundation

Printed and bound in Canada by Marquis
This book is printed on Enviro paper

Cover image: Margie Buckley, 1918. Glenbow Archives, NA-3017-4.
Copyediting by Alison Jacques
Cover design, page design, and typesetting by Melina Cusano

To the memory of Edith Ings (1880–1972)
and Constance Loree (1919–2009),
the first and second generation of ranch women in our family,
who inspired through their commitment and spirit of adventure.

And to my mom,
Linda Loree (1946–2014),
for her example of how to live wisely and with strength.
This work would not have happened without her
constant encouragement and wise editing.
All my love.

Table of Contents

Illustrations

Introduction: Women on the Ranching Frontier

On a frosty foothills morning in the early 1900s, shouts of "Ride 'em, LaGrandeurs" pierced the chill air.[1] Two riders, one with skirts flapping, rode out the bucking of their frisky mounts before galloping off toward home, much to the delight of the cheering friends they had just left behind at a barn dance.[2] Violet LaGrandeur's life story, punctuated by independent triumphs and the literal and figurative bruises that come from hard falls, is only one of many that can be told about women who rode, ranched, and raised families in the grasslands of the Canadian West. Despite the significance of their contributions, and women's undeniable presence on the range from the earliest frontier period to the present, studies focusing on ranch women are noticeably absent from the historiography of the West. Farm women, however, have been widely historicized; from depictions of a life of drudgery to the image of the selfless helpmate, they have been cast in a supportive role in the settlement of the prairies. Their involvement in the development of agricultural communities as well as the challenges and accomplishments in their lives have been recognized in a range of articles and monographs.[3] In contrast, extant histories of ranching frontiers have been dominated by research that perpetuates the myth of the cattle industry as a masculine realm. In most analyses, ranchers are assumed to be men, while their wives, mothers, sisters, and daughters are given cursory treatment. Too often, the early range men's business endeavours are dissected and their "cowboying" exploits glorified, creating an image of an entirely male-dominated pioneer cattle industry. This book intends to write ranch women into western history. It argues that the ranching frontier was not "hell on horses and women," but an environment that fostered women's resourcefulness and independence and in turn led them to transcend the restrictions of traditional gender roles and participate as active and essential players in the emerging cattle industry in Alberta.[4]

This study was largely motivated by my attempts to reconcile what I knew about my family's lived experience, on the one hand, with the history of the Alberta frontier that I encountered in books and popular culture, on the other. My family has ranched in Alberta since the 1880s. Independent and capable women have played a role in maintaining and sustaining our family ranch – as comfortable on a horse as they were in the kitchen – and I know the same is true on neighbouring outfits. As the fourth generation to ranch and raise a family here, I am certain that although technology has changed and shaped important aspects of our lives, the rhythms and routines of ranch life remain unchanged for many women. What I knew of my great-grandmother and what I saw my grandmother and her sister accomplish led me to believe that everyone acknowledged that women were, and are, integral to the success of family ranches. What I encountered in books and in the history courses I took at university, however, told a different story. Ranching women were largely invisible. The early women who helped to settle the province had homesteaded and farmed, I read; they fed threshing crews, grew gardens, and raised large families. But what of my great-aunt Mary, who taught me to work a cow from horseback when I was eleven and she was eighty? What of the "guest book" (favourite reading at our summer ranch) that told of the girls' riding to the hills in the 1920s to bring home the strays in the fall? What of the photographs my granny showed me in her kitchen, scented by rising bread dough, that depict her mother mounted and ready to start sorting the herd for branding? And Granny, age five, bundled on a pony and ready to ride to the one-room Sunset School, her *tapaderos*[5] dragging in the snow? These images did not connect to those I encountered in popular culture, of the rugged and solitary men who were said to live and ride hard as they established the cattle industry in the West. As I pursued my academic goals, began my own family and cattle herd, and became more aware of the living ranching

0.1 A young Constance Ings, the author's grandmother, riding her pony Daffy to Sunset School (c.1924). Courtesy of Loree family.

culture around me, it seemed timely and appropriate for me to bring to light the realities of the many ranching women in Alberta's past.

While the curiosity that fuelled this research was driven by my personal family history and my own sense of place within a ranching community, the theoretical framework of this study is shaped by the influences of scholars working within the field of western women's history, and particularly those concentrated in the study of the ranchers' West. Writing "herstory" had preoccupied many scholars in the 1980s when western women's history began to flourish.[6] Currently, both Canadian and American historians continue to grapple with the complexities of women's experiences on the western frontier – a concept fraught with symbols and ideologies that has long integrated myths of nation-building with constructions of masculinity. Historian Elizabeth Jameson still argues that "to add women to history will require us to separate the mythic Wests of both countries from history and to analyze how gender has functioned in them."[7] The frontier – with its associated connotations of conquest, patriarchy, and individualism – is a problematic term for revisionist western historians who have sought a more inclusive and complicated history of the West using race, class, and gender as necessary categories of analysis.[8] Despite this, the significance of the notion of the frontier endures.[9] This study considers the frontier as a fundamental component of its analysis, both as a concept and a region. When its accompanying myths of masculinity are deconstructed, the frontier represents unknown potentials for both men and women. The frontier, as it pertains to this analysis of southern Alberta, was the liminal "social process" involved in creating new settlement and refers to a specific natural environment dominated by grasslands that had yet to be understood by those who sought to put it into agricultural production.[10] Gender, another essential concept for this study, was, like the frontier, socially and culturally constructed and particular to time and place.[11] Thus, as men and women adapted to the conditions of the frontier and the patterns and expectations of their lives changed, their experience of gender and gender-specific roles evolved as well.

Within the field of ranching history, as historian Sarah Carter observes, some earlier works, including those by Sheilagh Jameson and Lewis Thomas, examined the lives of women, but few focused on the role of women in the cattle industry and ranching culture.[12] In a 1997 article, Carter argues that "a cherished myth of an entirely masculine ranching culture and cattle industry has proven difficult to dislodge. . . . It has been only through the highly selective use of evidence that the idea of a masculine ranching culture has been created and sustained."[13] While some myths about the West have been dismantled, the impression that the cattle frontier was an overwhelmingly male domain persists. Undeniably, men outnumbered women on this frontier. In the Macleod district, at the heart of ranching country, even as late as 1911, there were 18,231 male residents and only 12,548 females.[14] This gender disparity only increases when comparing single men with single women; in the same area in 1901, unmarried men outnumbered unmarried women by nearly two to one.[15] The preponderance of young men on the ranching frontier explains why they have been the central figures in its history, but it does not justify why the women who were there have largely been ignored. Images of the romantic role of the capable cowboy and the notion of a frontier existence where only the rugged individualist thrived have subsumed the reality: that early ranchers worked ceaselessly to adapt their agricultural methodologies to the environment and that their success often depended on cooperation with women within a family unit.

The research that sustains this close examination of ranching women and their families focuses on previously overlooked "evidence" to convey a fuller and more inclusive picture of ranching in southern Alberta. Reviewing the abundance of material artefacts, along with photographic and textual evidence, pertaining to ranch women effectively dismantles the illusion that they were not active participants in the formative years of the cattle industry. Many barns on ranches, some owned by the same families for over a hundred years, hold worn vintage saddles that are a testament to the miles women rode on the range. Photographs tucked into tattered albums display resourceful-looking women forking hay to cattle, or posed in front of well-maintained ranch houses surrounded by children, or confidently mounted on long-legged horses flanked by hounds and ready to hunt. From the frontier days onward there is a rich record of women on the range. This analysis of their daily lives conveys the complexities and realities of their existence and strengthens the understanding of their role in the ranching industry. Another purpose of this project is to give voice to the many women whose stories are known only to their families or immediate communities.[16] Several interviews with descendants of pioneer ranchers are included to bring these stories to light. Ranch women wrote. They used letters to bridge the distance between their isolated homes and the families they had left behind, they kept diaries to help process and record the daily events of their lives, and they wrote poetry and prose in response to a lifestyle and a landscape that were inspirational. Many wrote memoirs as a way to preserve what they felt had been a significant past. I have taken great pleasure in drawing liberally from women's writing and memories. There is no better way to understand women's experiences than through their own words.

A re-examination of the ranchers' West through the lens of a gender historian promises to provide a much-needed perspective on the most prevalent and persistent form of livestock raising – the family ranch. To date, historians have examined the Canadian ranching industry with great scope, but have merely hinted at the presence of women. Most commonly, ranching histories study the successes and failures of the large-scale open-range ranches that predominantly reigned over the "cattle kingdom" from the 1880s to the turn of the twentieth century. Among the first to focus on the society of the ranching West was Lewis Thomas, who proposed that Old World values and traditions were transplanted in the frontier by a community of privileged ranchers who created a society that reflected their British and Eastern Canadian heritage but was unique to Alberta.[17] Among the beliefs that endured, argues Thomas, was the notion that women were best suited to the domestic sphere and thus had a limited role on ranches other than being wives and mothers. In his exhaustive examination of the institutional foundations of its origins, historian David Breen depicts a cattle fraternity dominated by powerful men, motivated by financial gain and supported by political ambition.[18] In this context, where cattle ranching was considered big business, not a family economy, women played an incidental role. Both Thomas and Breen depict the Canadian range and its social institutions as distinct from those of the American cattle frontier. In contrast, however, by focusing on the daily routines and rhythms that defined and shaped rancher's lives in the Canadian West, the research and anecdotes that unfold in the following pages demonstrate how the frontier had a transformative effect on settlers' values, particularly concerning the status of women on ranches that were founded not on the principles of monopoly capitalism, but on the efforts of the family as a cooperative economic unit.

My work is more closely aligned with that of scholars Terry Jordan and Warren Elofson, who both cite environmental factors and the particular circumstances of caring for livestock as the most important factors influencing the development of cattle cultures. Jordan's close analysis of the transmission of ranching practices throughout North America illustrates that these practices, like the cattle themselves, crossed political boundaries.[19] Similarly, Elofson argues that the cattle culture of the northwestern Great Plains was similar on both sides of the American-Canadian border.[20] In particular, he details how, following the failure of the open-range ranches, small and mid-size ranchers adapted their practices to better suit the geographic and climatic features of the region. Building on these works, this study examines women's contributions on moderately sized ranches that adopted labour-intensive practices resembling those on mixed farms in order to ensure their sustainability. This study is focused on the ranchlands of southern Alberta, an area that reaches roughly from the Bow River south to the American border and from the foothills of the Rocky Mountains east to the short-grass prairies that surround the Cypress Hills. However, the analysis of Canadian ranch women is supplemented and complemented by research on their American counterparts. A similar material and social culture developed on both sides of the border. It was unique to ranching communities and changed from the culture that immigrants had left behind in the East.

The time frame of this study corresponds with the introduction of the first cattle herds, in the 1880s, and uses 1930 – a year that ushered in economic and climatic extremes – as a loose end date. It illustrates women's presence in the earliest frontier period and examines their continually expanding roles on family ranches, which became prolific after the turn of the century. For the sake of this study, the term "ranch" applies to any agricultural operation that was primarily invested in livestock, be it cattle, horses, or, more rarely in Alberta, sheep. Distinct from farms whose major commodity was grain, and from homesteads that were largely subsistence-based, the typical ranch raised beef cattle. Women were particularly indispensable on family-run ranches, where their productive and reproductive labour sustained their families and contributed directly to the viability of the operation. Although Linda Hussa is writing of the modern family ranch, her observation applies to the frontier ranch as well: "I know of no other industry that turns totally within the concentric circles of family and community."[21] It is women who were, and who remain, at the centre of those circles, mediating between the private and public spheres of home and economy. Each individual within a family unit was essential to the endless work involved on a ranch; women and children were integrated into the cycle of the operation that encompassed aiding birth, sustaining life, and acknowledging the certainty of death. As such, lines of gender division were blurred. For the young, the freedom

0.2 Josephene Bedingfeld feeding the hens on her family ranch (1915). Reproduced with permission of Glenbow Archives.

and responsibilities associated with frontier existence were particularly egalitarian. In his analysis of childhood in the American West, historian Elliott West notes that "sons did women's work, and far more often, young girls moved into the realm of men – herding, harvesting, and hunting."[22] As traditional gender roles broke down within the family, they became more flexible in the larger ranching community that both depended on and supported the family ranch. Along with their involvement in managing cattle on the range, women remained fundamentally responsible for the domestic sphere and the activities that went on in the home and barnyard. Despite the weight of their responsibilities in the home and the significance of their subsistence production, as Elizabeth Jameson adroitly articulates, "we still have histories of the cattle frontier, but not of the egg or butter frontiers."[23] The aim of this book is to encompass the feminine frontier to reflect the diversity and routines that defined the lives of ranch women within the home and on the range.

For the sake of specificity, this book primarily examines the experiences of women of European descent. Within ranching districts, the earliest immigrants dedicated to ranching were largely of Anglo origin. Those whose roots were in Eastern Canada, Britain, and the United States made up the relatively homogeneous dominant ranching order. Many women, conscious of their origins, explicitly identified whom they considered to be good neighbours. Elizabeth Sexsmith, who later married American cattleman George Lane, represented a commonly held pioneer perspective when she reflected that soon after her family had immigrated to the High River area in 1883, "the country began to settle quickly with good Scotch, English, Eastern Canadian people all farming, ranching, selling, and buying."[24] In his somewhat glossy account of early southern Albertan ranching communities, Thomas proposed that the typical ranching family was young and relatively well-funded.[25] In general, this was the case. Most ranching families initially came west with some means of establishing themselves comfortably, if simply, and providing for their daily needs. As Agnes Skrine of the Bar S Ranch (writing under her pen name, Moira O'Neil) attested of the ranching region in the 1890s: "No one is rich here. On the other hand, hardly anyone is distressingly poor, of those at least who live on their ranches like ourselves, and make their money by horses and cattle."[26] There were, however, many settlers who were indisputably poor and suffered a harsher existence than the typical ranching family, not to mention the less-typical families whose wealth placed them in an enviable position among their peers. The majority of ranchers were reasonably well educated and had enough funds to establish themselves and furnish a simple home, but they had to work and manage their assets carefully in order to maintain a viable ranch.

Although this study emphasizes the experiences of white women, Indigenous women were among the first female ranchers in both Canada and the United States, often marrying non-Aboriginal partners and holding active roles on frontier ranches.[27] Largely ignorant of Indigenous women's culture and their role in enabling the settlement of the plains, Anglo ranch women considered themselves to be the first women in the West and were dismissive of the contributions of their Aboriginal counterparts.[28] In Canada, most interactions between whites and First Nations peoples occurred when travelling bands or family groups camped near or on land recently claimed by ranchers. As scholar Sheila McManus notes, white frontier ranch women used their gender to position themselves as superior to First Nations women, but it was also their own "ambiguous positions . . . as subordinates in colonial hierarchies" that made them "fear aboriginal people and the spaces they dominated."[29] Once white women had overcome their initial fears of the "real red Indian," they often came to view them as novelties and regarded their visits, as Mary Daley did in 1889, as "a break in the routine . . . though sometimes a nuisance."[30] In some cases, white women recognized the female companionship of their First Nations visitors and welcomed them into their homes despite cultural and language barriers. Violet LaGrandeur recalled that as a young bride during a particularly lonely winter, "I was almost in tears baking bread, etc. when the kitchen door slowly opened and behold . . . there was another woman, a squaw. She could not speak a word of English but I could have embraced her. We got along very well by making signs. I made tea and we had some fresh bread."[31] Women of European descent enjoyed privileged status on the frontier in part because of their gender, in a region where men outnumbered women almost two to one, and in part because of their perceived cultural superiority over the dispossessed Aboriginal peoples. The social and geographical parameters of this study are limited to examining the pioneer experience. This specificity is meant to serve as a starting point in the discussion of women ranching in southern Alberta, while recognizing gender as a tool of colonialism. My hope is that it will open up the discussion for further, more nuanced analysis of Indigenous women in agriculture.

Pioneer women were attracted to the frontier for many of the same reasons as men. The potential of accessible land and economic independence encouraged settlers who were motivated by the opportunities the West offered. In addition, unmarried women came west optimistic about the prospects for employment and marriage in a region where women were in short supply. Some women, like Edith Scatcherd, were tempted to move west by a combination of persuasive partners and the allure of adventure. Scatcherd's husband-to-be, already an established rancher in southern Alberta, used the promise of a fast horse to sweeten the deal when encouraging her to leave Ontario to be with him. In one of his many letters, he wrote persuasively:

> I met a friend of mine [a few days] ago when I was shipping some stock from Cayley a short distance from here. I was riding my sweetheart's chestnut and he was so taken with her that he urged me to put a price on her. But I said no, said she belonged

0.3 THE WELL-APPOINTED MIDWAY RANCH AS IT WOULD HAVE APPEARED UPON THE ARRIVAL OF EDITH INGS (NÉE SCATCHERD) IN THE WEST (C.1910). COURTESY OF LOREE FAMILY.

> to one who was very dear to me. I do hope you will like her. But perhaps my little girl will not like any part of her surroundings myself included. But I think she is made of the right material and will soon realize that there are greater opportunities in this part of the world than the east.[32]

Despite the advantages promised by ranching, some women were "reluctant pioneers" who accompanied their husbands to the frontier out of obligation rather than enthusiasm.[33] Understandably, a fear of the unknown and the uncertainties of establishing oneself in a region far removed from the support of family and friends were psychologically daunting.

Even for those willingly engaged in the process of emigration, the transition could yield unpredictable challenges that tested a woman's fortitude. In 1909, Mary Nichols arrived on the southeastern prairies of Alberta accompanied by seven sons, whose ages ranged from three to twenty-one years.[34] Her husband, travelling by freight car with their livestock and the cash from the sale of their land in North Dakota, was to meet them several days later. Nichols had yet to locate their homestead when a telegram arrived notifying her that her husband had died of "heart trouble" en route.[35] When his body, the cattle, and their household possessions arrived the next day, the cash box was empty. Although never confirmed, the family suspects that he was murdered, with the money as motivation, after unloading the stock for water. Nichols's story demonstrates the resiliency of some frontier ranch women. She walked the seventeen miles to the 960 acres she claimed with her dependent sons and carried on. In a straightforward letter she wrote to friends back in North Dakota, briefly relating the events of her husband's death, she closed with "You folks had aught to come here and get land it surely is fine land. I can't think of much else to write now."[36] Fortified by her sons who worked adjoining land, Nichols ranched in the area until the 1920s, when she relocated to Turner Valley. As a testament to her contribution to her community, the Mary Nichols Dam just outside of Seven Persons, Alberta, bears her name.[37] Women in the ranchers' West – whether they were fortunate, like Scatcherd, who had arrived to a fine home and a doting husband, or not, like Nichols, who had arrived to heartache and hard work – were afforded unprecedented opportunities. Many of them met the challenges presented with resourcefulness and fortitude.

This book demonstrates how women responded to the new social and physical environment of the ranching frontier. It opens by showing that independent women played a more significant role in the early cattle industry than has previously been recognized. An extensive study of the family ranch argues that women's efforts contributed to the success and sustainability of this form of ranching. Following this examination of women's work is an exploration of evolving gender roles within the family and on the range. An analysis of the changes in ranch women's fashion and the saddles they used uncovers physical evidence of women's emancipation. Pioneer women's experiences of childbirth, which were discussed with surprising frankness in primary documents, are an important part of this analysis; they illuminate the women's fears, strength, and sense of community. Finally, an appreciation of the role of the horse as both a mode of mobility and a vehicle for equality rounds out the analysis. The conclusion illustrates how an intimate relationship with the land shaped women's sense of place and created within them a deep and lasting connection to a lifestyle and livelihood that has so often been construed as a man's world.

0.4 An open-range roundup – big sky, big herds, and riders working on horseback (1898). Reproduced with permission of Glenbow Archives.

As historian Lewis Thomas aptly notes, "it was the work of the ranchers that gave their community meaning."[38] For ranch women, it was often this work that defined their lives and gave structure to their days. Some scholars have deemed the burden of labour borne by ranching women oppressive and demeaning. Alternatively, women's productive and reproductive labour on ranches can also be viewed as a direct means of liberation. In her study of Manitoba farm women, Mary Kinnear notes that despite their unbelievable workload and a lack of "conveniences," many women were satisfied with their lives because they felt that they were "true partners" with their husbands.[39] In my research, this was also the case for ranch women who worked within relationships of mutuality with their partners. Most fundamentally, ranch work integrated with the seasons to demarcate the cyclical nature of women's lives: calving marked the return of spring and new optimism, the flurry of summer tasks took place against a backdrop of green grass and growing crops that then plunged into a frenzied fall of harvest and weaning, and then a retreat into winter gave families a chance to reconnect within the home. On top of this, the many opportunities for equal, independent work alongside their male counterparts gave ranching women a context in which to challenge the notions of Victorian domesticity that had been entrenched in society since the early nineteenth century. Western women were part of a larger emerging movement toward the recognition of female equality and capability. The frontier provided a social and physical environment in which women could experience the full capacity of their minds and bodies and realize personal emancipation. The degree to which women's status was enhanced by ranch work and their contributions recognized by their partners or the ranching community at large differed from family to family and from circumstance to circumstance. Mary Guenther, a third-generation rancher who raised her family and ran the operation after her husband's death in 1959, best described the challenges of depicting women's roles on ranches as she related her family history:

> You know, I think I've probably been giving the impression that ranch women are much more equal and involved and so on today, but I've been thinking back and I think women on farms and ranches have always done what needed to be done. There are an awful lot of women who didn't just cook for the threshing crews but worked in the field and milked ten cows and drove teams and whatever, so, you know, it's just that it is more official today or recognized or acknowledged possibly. I don't think people have changed that much. Circumstances change somewhat and ways you do things but I think there's always been very strong women.[40]

This book intends to tell their stories.

CHAPTER ONE

Independent Women Ranchers in an Emerging Industry

The majority of extant histories concerned with the early days of cattle ranching on the northern Great Plains focus on men's labour and investment in the region. They emphasize the fiscal speculation that drew men with means and political power to invest in the early cattle industry and the sense of adventure and opportunity that pulled young cowboys and would-be ranchers to the West. Though cattle ranching was predominantly a masculine endeavour, it was not just men who sought to capitalize on the opportunities of the open range. In addition to operating ranches in partnership with their husbands, numerous women owned stock independently, and their experiences have gone largely unexamined. It is critical, however, to define what is meant by the terms *women's autonomy* and *independence* in the context of the working ranch. As historian Dee Garceau explains, being independent did not necessarily mean living and working on the land alone – although occasionally this was the case and some women achieved "economic self-support."[1] Ranching was most effectively carried out by a family enterprise working within the context of a supportive community. When women worked as part of a ranching family, "independence meant economic viability as a family unit" or "decision making power within a group enterprise."[2] Examining a selection of women's accounts of their experiences as the owners and managers of ranches and stock in early cattle-grazing districts reveals that scholars have been remiss in discounting women's role and establishes ranch women's historical significance. Women were effective players in the early cattle industry and their engagement in the business of raising beef increased their personal sense of autonomy and their status within cattle communities on the western frontier.

The ranching industry in the western grasslands region began as a deliberate response to a market-driven demand for food, both locally and internationally. In western Canada – then known as the North West Territories – the presence of the first North-West Mounted Police (NWMP) troops in 1874, an influx of trappers and prospectors, and the dispossession and patronization of First Nations populations created a need for a productive provisions industry.[3] The success of grazing cattle south of the border and the increasing pressure due to high stocking rates on American ranges encouraged a northward movement of stock, while at the same time capital investment moved westward from major centres in England, Ontario, and Quebec. Due to the topographical and ecological similarity of the fescue grasslands of Montana and the region that is now southern Alberta and Saskatchewan, the first stock owners viewed the Canadian range as an untapped extension of the American livestock frontier. Small stockmen, many retired from service with the NWMP, were encouraged by the perceived potential for immediate sustained profit and introduced the first herds of cattle into the area in the mid-1870s.[4] Operating on a manageable scale with minimal investment and small herds, the earliest open-range ranchers proved that there was profit to be made by raising grass-fed beef on the northwestern plains. It was not only men who decided to capitalize on the opportunity presented by the newly opened cattle-grazing territory; several women are known to have participated in the earliest days of the cattle industry.

Though the cattle frontier promised wealth, this potential was accompanied by the risk of the unknown and the instability of a sparsely populated place. Despite the hazards involved, many women knowingly accepted these insecurities and invested their money and lives in cattle ranching. One of the first domestic cattle herds brought across the border from Montana in 1875 was owned by a husband and wife, but the "herd was always known as Mrs. Armstrong's" and the cattle were solely her responsibility and occupation.[5] She ran a dairy on the Old Man River north of Fort Macleod and her cattle were included in the first roundup conducted in the district, in 1879. At that gathering Mrs. Armstrong's interests were represented by her hired hand, Morgan. Though some of the first herds thrived and multiplied on the Canadian range, they were threatened by various factors such as weather, cattle rustling, and the near-starvation conditions that prompted the First Nations population to slaughter beef as a means of survival. Frustrated by the loss of substantial numbers of cattle, some stock owners decided to retreat south of the border. After reported losses to her herd following the roundup and having one of her cows shot through the head while penned in her corral, Mrs. Armstrong chose to move her herd back to Montana, where she and her hired man were subsequently murdered.[6] Similar hazards faced those who began the earliest ranches in the United States. Agnes Morley Cleaveland and her two younger siblings accompanied their widowed mother into the wilds of New Mexico, where they invested their inheritance to establish a cattle ranch. Frontier conditions typical on both sides of the border plagued the Morley family's endeavours, and though their ranch was a substantial size they barely managed to stay solvent. Cleaveland remembers how challenging it was for her mother:

> Faced with the supervision of a well-stocked cattle range of a good many thousand acres, she rode and did her indomitable best to keep herself informed about what was happening to her livestock; but she was unable successfully to cope with the cattle-rustlers who abounded and with the proclivities of open-range cattle to wander. . . . That she survived the years that followed speaks volumes for her courage, her stamina, and her self-sacrifice. It would have been so very easy to sink under the all but overwhelming flood of hardships and disappointments that were hers.[7]

Mrs. Armstrong's and the Morleys' experiences in the earliest stages of the cattle industry demonstrate that women participated in the same business endeavours and faced the same challenges as their male counterparts. The fledgling industry and the open range of the Canadian West held the same promise of opportunity for both men and women, but the conditions of the frontier and the tragedies and hazards it held were equally indiscriminate.

In Canada the unstable advent of the ranching industry was followed by a period of intense growth: herd sizes expanded, capital investments increased, and government interest in the West rose. Increased law enforcement by the NWMP, the promise of a transcontinental railroad, and the federal government's commitment of secure grazing rights encouraged serious investment in the cattle industry. The year 1881 marks the beginning of the "golden age" of the cattle kingdoms, when the Conservative government approved a lease system that enabled regulation of the large tracts of land used specifically for stock grazing.[8] By 1885, the reach of the railroad into the ranchlands had increased market opportunities for cattle ranchers. This period is infamous for cronyism on the part of major investors and famous for the integral role played by increasingly skilful cowboys. The fact that some women also participated and prospered in the early cattle business, acting as both owners and operators of ranches and not merely as helpmates to their husbands, is little known. As interest grew in the new frontier that stretched north from the American border and west from the prairies of central Canada, the belief that the cattle country was a decidedly masculine realm emerged. In the popular consciousness, and in academia, the stories of independent women ranchers have been subsumed by analyses of the ranching moguls and the exploits of the cowboys they employed. Feminist scholar Catherine Cavanaugh argues that "in constructing and reconstructing the West – from wilderness wasteland to economic hinterland to agrarian paradise – expansionist discourse perpetuated the myth of the west as a 'manly' space, assigning to it a moral and political force that underwrote elite Anglo-Canadian men's hegemony in the territories."[9] The same emphasis on the masculine nature of the frontier was propagated in the United States by the conventions of historian Frederick Jackson Turner's thesis that promoted individualism and viewed each new landscape and wilderness area as territory available for domination by men and their economic endeavours.[10] Esteemed American historian Walter Prescott Webb stated that "in the final analysis the cattle kingdom arose at that place where *men* began to manage cattle on horseback."[11] Despite this proscriptive ideology, many women bucked convention and sought to profit by using the resources of frontier environments. As Cavanaugh writes, "while the possibilities for women (and men) were shaped by masculinist cultural context, in the shifting realities of the turn-of the century, Euro-Canadian women's responses to cultural constructions of the West as a manly space were neither inevitable nor always predictable."[12] As the example of successful small-scale rancher Agnes Bedingfeld demonstrates, the "golden age" was not merely a period of huge ranches sustained by the myth of frontier masculinity and individualistic male enterprise; women working in cooperation with their community were also able to prosper in the emerging industry.

Despite the efforts of the large ranchers to keep the range open exclusively for grazing, squatters and homesteaders began to infiltrate the grasslands of the Canadian West as soon as it became known as a cattle region. In 1883, Agnes Bedingfeld squatted in prime ranching territory near the enormous Bar U Ranch on Pekisko Creek, southwest of what is now High River, Alberta. As a widow, she was able to use her status as the head of her household to acquire a homestead, which became the headquarters of the productive ranch she operated in partnership with her son, Frank. Together they developed a successful horse and cattle business and became well-respected members of the ranching community, even garnering the support of the largest ranchers in the area as they sought to expand their land base.[13] Bedingfeld's shrewd management of the ranch business led to the steady development and expansion of their infrastructure and herds. Her business aptitude was complemented by their combined competence in daily ranch operations and supplemented by her employment as a cook at the Bar U and Frank's as a cowboy. In spite of Bedingfeld's financial success, however, historian Henry Klassen points out that – in comparison with the displays of wealth shown by other ranchers, such as Pat Burns – "for Agnes Bedingfeld, ranching was not mainly an opportunity to pile up riches. . . . [R]ather than seeking to parade her wealth, Agnes tried to blend into the picturesque landscape. Famous for making her ranch an inviting place, she was adept at building and maintaining friendships in the Pekisko ranching community."[14] Unlike the cattle corporations, Bedingfeld was intent on building a home, not just a business. Women's vested interest and labour were a constant factor in the success of this small-scale ranch. Bedingfeld provided the initial capital and the consistent management of the ranch, and she ran the operation independently while her son went to the North to prospect for gold in 1898 and 1899. Frank's wife, Josephene, later ran the ranch while he spent two years overseas during World War I. Like her mother in-law, "she [Josephene] was a splendid rider and negotiated many successful horse sales during her husband's absence."[15] By the

1.1 Mrs. Agnes K. Bedingfeld and Frank Bedingfeld. Together, mother and son established a reputable, successful ranch in prime cattle country (c.1900–03). Reproduced with permission of Glenbow Archives.

time the 1,600-acre ranch was sold to the Prince of Wales in 1919, it was a reputable and profitable example of the competence and commitment of women in the early ranching industry.[16]

By the turn of the century, the rate of settlement had intensified in both ranching and farming regions in western Canada. The federal government used promotional propaganda and the promise of free land to entice settlers to the agricultural regions of the prairies. However, the ideology accompanying the Dominion Lands Act of 1872 held that men alone were fundamentally inclined to be productive agriculturalists. The restrictive decree of Canadian homestead laws dictated that women were permitted to obtain land only if they were the heads of households, which, in interpretation, basically meant only widows with dependent children under the age of twenty-one. As minister of the interior Clifford Sifton elucidated in 1905, "the department does not recognize the right of a woman to take up homesteads."[17] It was this gender-biased decree that most fundamentally challenged the notion of "the frontier-as-equalizer."[18] As Cavanaugh argues, the prevention of access by single women to homestead land, combined with the failure of early women's campaigns to win married women equal rights to their property, reveals an element of "patriarchy preserved on the prairie."[19] The gender-biased system inhibiting single women from claiming agricultural land overlooked two important factors that should have influenced policymaking: one, the premise of the argument in this chapter, that women who were able to access land proved to be capable as independent agricultural producers; and two, that south of the border the American Homestead Act was granting women "free" agricultural land and that these women were highly successful in creating homes, farms, and ranches in the West.

While government rhetoric discouraged women from becoming agriculturalists, many women viewed pioneering as a way to improve their lot in life. Following a trip to Canada to observe the realities of pioneer life in the early 1900s, English author Mrs. Cran was dismayed to find few "bachelor" women working the land. She mused, "Travelling as I am doing at this stage of my visit, week in and week out, over soil so rich, I am constrained to wonder if there is any reason why women should not come out and work it as well as men."[20] Cran posited that for the "appropriate" woman, homesteading or the outright purchase of agricultural land promised opportunities unimaginable in the Old World: "women in England have no conception of the openings there are for them in the great North-West. Given health and industry, there is a fortune waiting them in that marvellous prairie loam, just as surely as for the men who go out to grow wheat and run stock-farms."[21] If Cran had travelled in the American West she would have encountered many more women working and living on land held in their own name. Due to a homesteading policy that was not biased in terms of gender, there are thousands of documented cases of female homesteaders south of the border. These American "girl homesteaders," historian Glenda Riley notes, even had a better rate of "proving up" than their male counterparts.[22] The personal observations of Elinore Pruitt Stewart, who established a ranch in Wyoming in 1909, spoke to the potential of women homesteaders:

> To me, homesteading is the solution of all poverty's problems, but I realize that temperament has much to do with success in

> any undertaking, and persons afraid of coyotes and work and loneliness had better let ranching alone. At the same time, any woman who can stand her own company, can see the beauty of a sunset, loves growing things, and is willing to put in as much time at careful labor as she does over the washtub, will certainly succeed; will have independence, plenty to eat all the time, and a home of her own in the end.[23]

Although published for an audience wanting to believe that the West afforded opportunity and egalitarianism, this depiction of the competent female homesteader resonates with the lived experience of women on both sides of the border; those who eschewed lives of domesticity and the security of established communities to engage themselves in the West proved to be as successful and as fulfilled as their male counterparts.

Despite the gender-biased nature of homesteading on paper and in government rhetoric, many Canadian women filed and proved up claims independently. Interestingly, multiple sources that suggest women claimed homesteads in their own names do not indicate the marital status of the women. It has to be presumed that the majority of these women would have been widows. Some widowed women, such as Agnes Bedingfeld, came west and started their ranches alone or with their children, while others continued the progress on their newly established ranches after their husbands had died. In their quest for land in the Lethbridge area in 1909, women householders were, for the most part, given equal treatment by their male counterparts even if at times "chivalry [was] not much in evidence."[24] On one occasion, three women were reported among a fighting mob of potential homesteaders outside the land office. According to pioneer Wilfrid Eggleston, who quoted from an item in the *Lethbridge Herald*, "'several big male brutes' impeded the progress of the women and one of the 'brutes' was observed deliberately holding back the women by the arm, so that a male could force his way in ahead of her."[25] Despite this instance, single women homesteaders typically garnered respect from their contemporaries and from those who recorded their experiences in local history books. Following her husband's death in 1893, Mrs. Murphy "took a homestead on the creek at Pincher and was known to be the first woman to do so in the community."[26] When widowed during the infamously cold winter of 1906–07, Mrs. Ford took over the family-run operation, negotiating with cattle buyers and improving the bloodlines of her horse herd by introducing the Shire breed. Apparently, "many farmers in the Nanton-Stavely district improved their power supply by buying horses from Mrs. Ford."[27] She became the legal owner of her ranch by inheritance, the most common way for women to circumvent the gender-biased homesteading process.

However they acquired their land, women proved successful as ranchers and independent operators of small-scale stock farms. They demonstrated the abilities integral to prospering in the developing cattle industry, including shrewd business sense, and the skill set necessary to run cattle, grow crops, and develop infrastructure. Adequate grazing land with shelter and a secure water supply was the most important asset for stock grazers. Female cattle-owners, like their male counterparts, were cognizant of the complexities associated with managing herds in increasingly populated areas. In the Nanton-Parkland district, Mosquito Creek was an important water source and became a cause of contention between ranchers and homesteaders who fenced the creek and ran off herds of open-range cattle from the water. Mrs. Ingram, who settled in the Parkland area to ranch with her two sons in 1901, understood the significance of water rights and resourcefully had each member of her family claim land along the creek. She demonstrated prudent foresight by taking advantage of homesteading laws to ensure their large herd of cattle had access to water.[28]

As early as 1887, women in the Calgary area were proving to be successful on their own small ranches and mixed farms. When one journalist surveyed the area along Pine Creek fifteen miles south of Calgary he found a number of women, both single and widowed, among the prospering agriculturalists. He reported that "about a mile from the trail Miss Wilkin owns a half section, which was purchased from Capt. Boynton, and she is bringing it into a good state of cultivation."[29] Another young woman, Miss Jerram, "has made especially good progress, and has a little band of cattle."[30] The reporter was particularly impressed by the rate of development on Mrs. Hudson's land:

> The first place we came to in the divide is that of Mrs. Hudson. She went in there four years ago [1883], when a long journey was needed to do much visiting of neighbors. A good deal of substantial fencing has been done, and a sturdy crop of grain is

> growing. She has a herd of between thirty and forty dairy cows and horses, which will be enlarged by a crop of probably twenty calves this year. We saw a very interesting book of watercolor paintings of prairie flowers, from the hands of Miss Lilly Hudson, very cleverly and beautifully painted.[31]

Women proved capable of not only establishing ranches, but maintaining them and keeping them viable. Many women did domestic work or cooked for their neighbours in exchange for having their farm work done or hired out the specialty jobs such as ploughing and seeding. However, some did the full spectrum of manual labour on their ranches themselves. In the Wood Mountain area in what is now Saskatchewan, another journalist reported on "the most industrial family I met there": a widow, Mrs. Chamberlain, and her teenage daughter, who were working to save their debt-ridden ranch after Mr. Chamberlain's death.[32] This mother and daughter duo handled all the daily operations, marketed their products, made improvements to the infrastructure, and, according to an eyewitness, could "rope a steer and ride a horse with any rancher in the country":[33]

> They have today about 275 head of cattle and 40 horses. . . . This summer they have milked 15 cows, filled the contract with the North West Mounted Police in the district for butter and had $150 worth of butter extra in their milk house ready to take to market. They cut with a mowing machine, raked up and drew in and stacked 100 loads of hay this summer for the use of their cattle. They branded 55 calves; they built an addition to the house, about 16x20, of lumber and shingles drawn from Moose Jaw, 120 miles distant, by themselves. They fenced in with a neat picket fence a garden of an acre in extent.[34]

This exhaustive list of undertakings indicates the scope of ranch women's accomplishments. Women did not shirk hard work, and they proved equal to the task of owning and operating ranches.

Even women who ranched not independently but in partnership with their husbands or families, were able to participate as owners in the cattle or horse business. Some women circumvented the rigid patriarchal system that prevented them from sharing the title of land with their husbands by assuming legal ownership of other commodities, including cattle and horses. The abolishment of dower by the Territorial Real Property Act of 1886 had effectively ensured that land, the major measure of wealth in an agricultural economy, was owned and controlled by men.[35] Even a series of amendments to Alberta's legislation earned by the early women's reform movement in 1917 failed to uphold a married woman's interest in the family estate. Ranch and farm women were not entitled to their share of the property and accompanying assets until the disappointing results of the landmark *Murdoch v. Murdoch* case in 1979 prompted a national feminist campaign that finally won equal property rights for married women.[36] However, a brand is an indisputable symbol of ownership; it is a virtually indelible mark that by 1900 was recognized by both range custom and government ordinance as verification of an individual's claim to specific stock. All of the lists of brand records in published local history books indicate that women held brands in their own names. According to Macleod district brand records from 1888 to 1913, women had registered 27 of 476 horse and cattle brands.[37] In the Stavely area from 1906 to 1918, women's brands numbered 11 of the 123 recorded in the local history.[38] A search of the extensive brand files at the Stockmen's Memorial Foundation Archives lists 151 brands registered to single and married women, both separately and with their husbands. These numbers are remarkable in the context of the patriarchal legal climate and considering that the demographic ratio in the same region at this time favoured men to women at approximately two to one.[39] Among the brands recorded in the Macleod district was a cattle brand belonging to Alice H. Mott. She and her husband had accompanied the 1886 Powder River Cattle Company drive from Wyoming to the North-West Territories. This drive had brought ten thousand head of cattle to the land that the ranch had recently purchased on Mosquito Creek. Upon their arrival, the Motts operated a stopping house and a moderately sized ranch. Mrs. Mott had two sources of income: running cattle and feeding travellers.

Women owned livestock under a variety of circumstances on the frontier. While Mott likely tended her own cattle with her husband, Evelyn Springett ran her stock on a range adjacent to the ranch managed by her husband, Arthur Richard Springett. Her "Circle Arrow" brand was applied to about eight or ten cows. She was proud of her ownership, writing

1.2 The capable Ings sisters, Mary and Constance, working their cattle at the Smith corrals, neighbouring their Trail's End Ranch (c.1930). Courtesy of Loree family.

that "A.R.S. as manager, did not care to own any cattle himself, but he allowed me to invest in a small herd."[40] Priddis-area rancher Monica Hopkins also owned her own stock. As her personal herd of horses (which had begun from one mare acquired as a wedding gift) began to expand, Hopkins remarked that "Billie says I shall soon have to apply for a brand of my own. Both my colts are fillys [*sic*] – isn't that lucky?"[41] She was well aware that a breeding herd was certain to multiply, in both physical numbers and capital worth. On the Rocking P Ranch in 1923, both of the owner's daughters, Maxine and Dorothy Macleay, owned stock; this was seen as a positive way to ensure one's children had a vested interest in the ranch.

The girls wrote, "Max and her 'pard' started in the horse business this month, with one colt apiece, branded as follows: Max, 3 on the right jaw; Dorothy, 5 on the left jaw."[42] The following month they acquired cattle: "Dorothy and her 'pard' started in the cow business this month. Max got a heifer branded [half diamond over] 5E on the left ribs. Dorothy captured a roan steer, also branded [half diamond over] 5E on the left ribs."[43]

Women profited by taking initiative and engaging themselves in the well-being of livestock. Being educated in how to handle stock and having the confidence to independently assert themselves in a critical situation sometimes provided them with a direct return on their efforts. One quick-thinking woman, Mrs. Sharples, the daughter of the manager of the "44" Ranch in the Porcupine Hills, demonstrated a rancher's characteristic initiative and was rewarded for it in the late 1890s.[44] Driving a wagon with her two babies on board en route to the "44," Mrs. Sharples came across a cow and calf stuck in a mud hole in a notoriously treacherous canyon. As her friend Evelyn Springett recalled,

> Though she realized that she was taking considerable risk in approaching any wild animal with young, she knew that, if they were left without help, they would probably both die. Being the plucky wife of a "cowman," she did not hesitate, though she confessed to me afterwards that she was terrified.[45]

After unloading her young children and putting them in a safe spot, Mrs. Sharples had hesitantly approached the unfortunate pair until she determined that they were indeed stuck fast in the mud. She proceeded to milk the cow into her shoe and then feed the hungry calf. After dragging the calf from the bog and putting it on dry ground, she continued on her way to the ranch. By the time ranch cowboys found the cattle the next day, the cow had died. The calf, however, lived and was given to Mrs. Sharples. Three years later she exported the animal to England and sold it at a profit.[46]

Another way women acquired stock was by caring for orphaned calves, lambs, or foals. These helpless animals required more attention than was deemed profitable by many cowboys and ranchers and so were often turned over to women, who cared for them in the barnyard. The poem "The Motherless Calf," written by rancher and poet Rhoda Sivell and published in 1911, depicts the pathetic state of an orphaned calf and the sympathetic response of a woman rancher:

> We put you away in the old cow's stall;
>
> And we made you warm and dry;
>
> We gave you milk of the best to drink,
>
> But we could not stop your cry.
>
> The little motherless heifer,
>
> Out in the old rough shed,
>
> Is the pick of the bunch with my pard and I,
>
> Because her mother is dead.[47]

Women's practical and maternal response to the needs of orphaned animals often yielded profitable results. Ann Clifford, who was married to the manager of the Bar U Ranch during the 1930s, saved an average of five lambs a season by bottle-feeding them and raised an orphaned filly named Lady who went on to raise seven foals.[48] However they acquired them, owning and caring for their own stock contributed to women's income and to their engagement and sense of personal interest in ranching operations.

The fictitious submissions in the "matrimonial bureau" of the handwritten *Rocking P Gazette* indicate that their teenaged, ranch-raised authors clearly understood the flexibility of gender roles and the opportunities made possible for them by women who lived and worked independently in ranching country. One of Dorothy and Maxine Macleay's presumably tongue-in-cheek "personal ads" reads as follows:

> A charming young lady wishes to correspond (view to matrimony) with good-looking Cowboy. Lady owns a small ranch; two cows and a pig; would like a cowboy capable of looking after stock, cooking, washing dishes, and all kinds of housework. Must be a HUSTLER – no lazy ones need apply.[49]

Despite the dominant belief that ranching was the domain of men, women proved equally capable and competent at venturing to the unsettled West, investing in the cattle business, and running profitable enterprises. Whether by operating their own ranches or maintaining herds of their own stock, women found ways to circumvent standards of convention, assert their independence, and increase their personal assets, despite the legal and social restrictions they faced. The cattle frontier afforded opportunities unknown to women in more established society. Those who successfully handled the workload and enjoyed the gamble of the livestock market could be formidable and enterprising players in the often unpredictable and male-dominated ranching industry.

CHAPTER TWO

The Family Ranch: Women in the Barnyard and Beyond

Despite myriad challenges and threats, such as unpredictable environmental conditions, periodic economic downturns, and market volatility, the family ranch has endured and remained viable for generations on the grasslands of southern Alberta. When the so-called great ranches established during the glorified golden age of the cattle kingdoms failed, smaller ranches that functioned primarily with the labour of immediate family took their place as the most prolific form of raising livestock. These moderate ranches were made sustainable by better adaptation to the environment, in terms of developing infrastructure and supplementary feeding programs, and by their manageable scale that often integrated mixed farming with extensive livestock grazing. However, this chapter will demonstrate that another significant and traditionally overlooked factor contributed to the success of smaller ranches. Women's integral labour enabled the family unit to persist as the most stable form of ranching. By working in partnership, husbands and wives were able to provide the close management necessary to establish and maintain businesses that could both meet the immediate needs of their families and sustain growth for future generations.

Before exploring women's direct contributions to the family ranch it is necessary to examine how this more intensive form of cattle raising came to be. The dominance of the family ranch coincided with the demise of many massive spreads during the early years of the twentieth century; moderately scaled, labour intensive, with the supporting infrastructure to protect their herds, family operations took over the range when the largest ranches failed.[1] The majority of large-scale open-range ranches that had initially dominated the region proved to be unsustainable and did not survive much past the open-range period and the turn of the twentieth century. As the pioneers of the industry soon discovered, ranching on the high plains and the foothills fescue regions required a modified system of livestock management and agriculture that combined established practices brought up from the United States with adaptations to suit the area's ecosystem and environment. The successful model that has persisted in Alberta, in the form of the family ranch, integrated the extensive grazing practices of the open-range ranches and the intensive management typically associated with the mixed farm.

The earliest and largest cattle operations, such as the Walrond Ranche and the Cochrane Ranche Company, used a system of livestock management that required minimal input costs but was unproven on the Canadian grasslands. As historian Warren Elofson points out, "On paper, ranching was a marvellous process. . . . [T]he animals would harvest the prairie grass while their owners did little more than watch and rake in the money."[2] The owners and managers of these great ranches turned massive herds out on vast ranges and virtually left the cattle to fend for themselves. In doing so, they overestimated the carrying capacity of the land when deciding on stocking rates and underestimated the severity of the northern climate. Cost-cutting measures – such as hiring minimal numbers of cowboys to oversee these herds and failing to stockpile enough hay and grain for supplementary winter feeding – exacerbated the loss of cattle and profits. Threats particular to the frontier, including predation, cattle rustling, and wandering stock, further contributed to financial losses. When combined with fiscal mismanagement and the vagaries of international export markets, these untried and subsequently inadequate management practices led to the downfall of the "great ranches." Even in typical years these ranches struggled to maintain their herds from season to season, but they found themselves drastically ill-equipped to protect and provide for the cattle during the extreme winter seasons of 1886–87 and 1906–07. While the winter of 1886–87 brought massive losses and served as a warning to the industry, it was twenty years later that the effects of another hard season combined with a failing export market to cripple the large corporations. As environmental historian Barry Potyondi asserts, the devastating winter of 1906–07 marked the inevitable end of the initial golden age of ranching.[3]

The myth of open-range ranching outlived the method. The era of large cattle corporations was actually an anomaly in western Canada; small stockmen had brought the first herds to the region, and small and medium-sized ranches continued to survive. As early as the late 1880s the family approach was established in the region and with close management – made possible by the vested interest of family members – was able to weather the literal and figurative storms that wreaked permanent havoc on the larger spreads. Smaller ranches far outnumbered large ones in the prime grazing areas. According to census reports, "between 1891and 1901, while two big ranches existed in the Bow Valley, the number of small ranches increased from 176 to 458, most of which had fewer than three hundred head of cattle."[4] According to historian David Breen, mid-size stock growers took over from the large corporations and were increasingly influential in industry organizations like the Western Stock Growers Association: "it was the 'new man' [*sic*] . . . who saved the western cattle export industry from threatened collapse after 1905."[5] It was not just this "new man," however, but also women and children who contributed to the successful transition into a more feasible form of cattle ranching.

There was a wide variation in the size of family ranches. The smallest, particularly in their earliest forms, stocked fewer than one hundred cows. Moderate spreads, like the Ings brothers' OH Ranch near Longview, ran approximately 600 head in the 1880s. In 1893, in the Macleod area, smaller ranches had stocking rates that ranged from 9 to as many as 650 head.[6] The Little Bow Cattle Company on Mosquito Creek – owned by a partnership that included Thomas and Adela Cochrane and managed by part owner (and Thomas's cousin) William "Billie" Cochrane and his wife, Evelyn – stocked 800 head of good quality Galloway-Hereford cross cattle in 1890.[7] Among the larger family-owned ranches, the Macleays' Rocking P had herds that at times numbered in the thousands.[8] Many ranchers started out with a homesteaded quarter section and used open range to graze their stock. Those with more financial backing operated on significant amounts of deeded land and access to rangeland. However, as the best grasslands became more densely settled and fenced toward the end of the 1890s most ranches operated with a combination of privately owned land and increasingly regulated grazing leases. In the early 1890s, "the leased land held by the average cattle operator fell from over 30,000 to just under 1,100 acres."[9]

Although their acreage was reduced, it was these leases that enabled most family ranches to continue, ensuring the continuation of some of the extensive grazing practices from the open-range period and enabling ranchers to maintain sizeable herds without overgrazing their home range.[10] The homeplace and ranch headquarters were typically used to winter the cattle and calve the cows in the spring, while in the summer months cattle were turned onto large areas of leased land on the hardy short-grass prairie in the eastern parts of the province, in the rich fescue of the foothills, or into the remote and rugged forestry of the mountains. The use of leased land and the necessity of mounted work that accompanied it is what primarily differentiated ranchers from mixed-farmers, who tended to keep smaller herds close to home year-round and managed their docile stock on foot. Isolation was also one of the main defining characteristics of frontier cattle ranches. Ranches were necessarily remote in order to allow enough room for animals to graze, and they were pushed into more marginal areas after 1900 with the flood of farmers and settlers into the region.[11] The use of large tracts of grazing land required ranch men and women to maintain the skill set for which the open-range cowboys were noted. Managing semi-feral stock on expansive ranges ensured that ranchers continued to ride and rope to manage their herds even as they now routinely laboured at less romantic work such as stacking hay and fixing fences.

By the 1900s most family-run ranches had begun to diversify their agricultural operations. The practices that persisted were in some ways more akin to mixed farming than to open-range grazing.[12] In his explicative 1913 text *The Range Men*, contemporary journalist L. V. Kelly described the drastic changes that had come to the cattle industry and envisioned what the industry was to become: "the future of it . . . is a gigantic mixed farm, stock fed throughout the winter, happy relations with farmers who take stock to feed."[13] To a degree his prediction rang true. Contrary to the mythologized notion that ranches could thrive with little input, to ensure the well-being of their stock, ranchers had to adopt practices that were labour intensive and involved some farming in order to supply additional

2.1 Myrtle Forster operating the binder, preparing grain for harvest (c.1913–19). Reproduced with permission of Glenbow Archives.

feed in the winter. What differentiated them from the typical homesteader, however, was that the size of their herds required access to large tracts of unbroken grassland. Even if their operations were exceedingly similar to those of their farming neighbours, many ranchers, particularly those who had participated in the glory days of the open range, held deep-rooted animosity toward farmers.[14] These ranchers resented the increased pressure "to break up [their] beloved sections of prairie land," as pioneer Robert Newbolt (Bob) articulated.[15] Even when they recognized the necessity of supplementary feeding, stock growers continued to ideologically privilege grassland over farmland. However, in order to survive, all ranchers had to relinquish some of their pride and any of the initial hostility they had held against farmers for fencing and ploughing up the prairie. Even "old-timers" like Newbolt, who cursed the intrusion of fences and tilled soil, became resigned to adopting farming practices and cross-fenced their ranches. Newbolt resisted change exceptionally late. In 1920 he reckoned,

> All my neighbors were out making dust. Why shouldn't I be making dust too [?] . . . The Bally farmers continued to move in and by this time my range was practically all fenced up. My friendly relations with my neighbors were not too good. I had to

> reduce my herds of both cattle and horses, also had to depend more on my farming operations for feeding my livestock.[16]

Unlike Newbolt, the majority of ranchers had adopted mixed-farming practices by the 1900s. Even the much-touted chinook winds did not render the prairie suitable for grazing 365 days a year. Even today, the few ranches that are forage based year-round have to closely manage their herds during the worst winter conditions, even going so far as to clear snow from the fields in order for the cattle to graze stockpiled grass that has been reserved specifically for the purpose.[17] According to census reports, hay-cropping increased dramatically between 1905 and 1910 as more ranchers fed stock through the cold season.[18] Particularly after the killing winter of 1906–07, most stockmen acknowledged that it was imperative to feed cattle throughout the winter months, thus increasing the ranchers' workload.

When they operated on a feasible scale, it was possible for ranchers to develop the infrastructure necessary to closely monitor and provide shelter for their animals. With part of the ranchlands now devoted to farming, fences had to be erected to protect the crops. Like the farmers, ranchers incorporated barbwire into their infrastructure. As Elofson notes,

> By 1901 fences had made district round-ups virtually impossible everywhere except south of Medicine Hat, here and there in the hills, along the Bow and Red Deer Rivers south east of Calgary, and in some districts of southern Assiniboia. At that time those who had not yet sufficiently divided up their lands were buying up wire – some by the "car load" – in an effort to get the job done.[19]

This made a significant change both to the range landscape and to the dynamics of running cattle and turned out to be a valuable and revolutionary management practice. The introduction of barbwire meant that it was suddenly feasible to erect miles of fenceline. Fences enabled ranchers to contain stock, making the animals easier to oversee, and proved invaluable for improving the breeding of range cattle. They kept neighbouring herds from mingling, segregated the bulls to allow for a more controlled

2.2 Margie Buckley feeding stockpiled forage to cattle (1918). Reproduced with permission of Glenbow Archives.

breeding season, prevented higher-quality breeding cows from mixing with range bulls, and restricted the herds' movement while directing them to shelter to prevent losses during severe weather. However, many of the innovations that made ranches more sustainable also created an increased workload. On top of the seasonal work associated with the cattle herd – including calving, branding, and roundup – now seeding, haying, and harvesting became part of the yearly cycle. Building infrastructure required not just an initial investment of time and money, but also, and inevitably, ongoing maintenance and attention. Caring for the more valuable purebred stock and dairy cows that tended to stay closer to home meant that the daily tasks associated with livestock care, like feeding and watering, became a part of the already busy barnyard routine. Close management was labour intensive and thus required all family members to contribute.

At the same time that a new order was taking over the ranching industry, an increasing number of women came west, and these women – wives, mothers, daughters, and sisters – became key contributors to the success of the family ranch. Labour was a valuable commodity on the frontier, where the sparse population, little established infrastructure, and the great distance between ranches meant there was always more work than there were bodies to do it. Thus, for both logistical and financial reasons, the bulk of work was performed by family members instead of hiring outside labour. The work was endless, particularly when homes and ranches were new, and could be loosely divided into three categories: domestic work that centred on the home, barnyard chores that were part of a daily routine, and ranch work at large that tended to the commercial livestock herd. All labour was so integrated with the communal good of the family and the family economy that the work of women and children was recognized to be as imperative as that of men. Women's and children's labour was considered integral to the ranch as a whole. In her analysis of farm families in the American Midwest, historian Mary Neth proposes that "wages, the factor that devalued women's labor in the market economy, did not define the value of work on a family farm. Daily, periodic, and seasonal tasks structured farm work and connected the rhythms of human needs to those of nature, the needs of the family to those of the farm."[20] This same pattern prevailed on family ranches in the Canadian West; thus, women and children capable of attending to a multitude of tasks and chores were valuable and valued assets on a working ranch. The family ranch functioned only because of the contributions of each of its members.

One fact about the ranching industry that has remained consistent throughout every period of history is that it was – and is – barely, rarely, and only occasionally profitable. Elofson bluntly argues that the family ranch has "endured in Alberta, Saskatchewan, and Montana largely because it is able to keep going in an industry which tends over much of the time to be uneconomic."[21] On top of the fact that beef markets have always been volatile, establishing a fully operational diversified ranch was costly. As one woman noted upon the completion of her family's outbuildings and corrals in the mid-1880s, "from our experience of this, building is still a very expensive amusement, and I think it would be cheaper to buy a ranche already well improved, than to do any building oneself."[22] Most ranches began as bare land and their infrastructure was built from scratch. Ranchers had to find ways to live affordably during times of little income and to create ways of building up their operations with little financial input. Families used different strategies to fund their ranches, but the work of family members always made the costly process more affordable.

Women's engagement with the primary production of raising beef for market – and their complementary labour – enabled ranches that had not overextended themselves in terms of debt load and stocking rates to survive despite the economic uncertainty of the industry. While ranching historiography in general has neglected the essential role of women on ranches, family histories frequently attest to the significance of women's labour in keeping ranches functional and viable. Local history books are laden with stories of hardworking women, written by family members who obviously respected and valued these women's contributions to their ranches. One strategy typical of pioneering families was to utilize the labour of all family members during the first few years of establishing a ranch. This was true of the Bonds when they first arrived in the West to ranch near Longview in 1899. Catherine Bond and her siblings spent the first three years at home rather than attending school because there was so much work to be done: "there were horses to ride, chores to do, cattle to herd."[23] While her labour was essential to the immediate well-being of her family's cattle operation, the skills that Bond acquired during her childhood also positioned her to be a valuable and equal partner to her husband when she joined him on his ranch along Willow Creek in 1914.[24]

The experience of the Austin family of the Pincher Creek area illuminates a pattern typical of many young ranch families and demonstrates how some couples pooled their resources to make their ranch a success. By working as a cowboy for the larger ranchers in the area throughout the 1890s, Fred Austin was able to acquire a homestead stocked with a few horses and cattle. His bride, Katherine, joined him in 1901. During the winter he worked for a lumber company in the Crowsnest Pass while she cared for their new baby, home, and livestock. Left alone to fend for herself, Katherine Austin resourcefully adapted to what needed to be done, even donning her husband's clothing so that the milk cow would accept her and stand for milking. Over the years the couple worked side by side, only expanding their operation at a rate they could manage together. Their primary income came from grazing beef cattle on the open range, but Katherine's production of milk, butter, and eggs paid for their taxes and living expenses. As a result of their combined efforts, the Austin family thrived and their Thornhill Ranch remained viable.[25] The following pages will further explore the pattern illustrated by the Austins' experience: that is, working off the ranch for wages or maintaining the ranch during a husband's absence, supplementing income by producing saleable goods on the ranch, conserving money by producing food, and involving oneself in ranching and farming activities – all were sustainable strategies through which women helped ensure the longevity of the family ranch.

Hiring out was a common way for families with meagre means to establish ranches, and the involvement of both partners made this practice possible. In some cases, married couples worked on established ranches together until they could afford to start one up on their own. Directly after their marriage in 1905, William and Annie Lane spent six months working on the C.Y. Ranch, he as a range rider and she as a cook. Annie's childhood had prepared her for working for a living. As a young woman she and her sisters baked and sold a hundred loaves of bread a day to supplement their family's income. Thus, prior to marriage she was accustomed to the reality that her labour contributed to the good of the entire family.[26] Large ranches, like the Macleays' near Nanton, continued to provide employment for couples who worked out together long after the frontier was considered closed. In 1924, the *Rocking P Gazette* noted that "Mr. Chuck cook, his wife and family have left the Bar S outfit. Their places were taken by Mr. and Mrs. Calkins."[27] Commonly, for those who owned their own spreads,

2.3 A glimpse of ranch reality. Note the baby in her arms, the chickens scratching in the yard, and the hog at the doorstep (c.1900–07). Reproduced with permission of Glenbow Archives.

a husband found temporary employment off the ranch, in lumber, mining, or freighting, while his wife kept the ranch operational during his absence. In the Pincher Creek area in the early 1900s, Johanne Pedersen was frequently left alone to care for the ranch and her seven children while her husband worked as a freighter. Alongside her many domestic chores, Pedersen was known to "stack hay, stook grain, clear land, saw wood by hand and brand calves."[28] When a woman had the skills and the resourcefulness to manage the ranch in the absence of her husband, it was feasible for him to earn the income they needed to build their spread from the ground up.

Alternatively, one of the most direct ways in which women enabled ranches to grow during the early years or to survive through financial hardship was by producing saleable products like eggs and butter. Extant ranching histories, more focused on the production of beef for commercial markets, have largely ignored the extent to which efforts in the barnyard contributed to a ranch's success. However, as Neth points out, "the connection between women's income and family purchases appears almost universal. . . . Women's labor and women's products proved vital sources of income as well as income-savers for family farms."[29] Like that of their farming counterparts, the additional income that ranch women provided through egg and dairy production sustained many families on the range. Proximity to a steady market, whether it be neighbouring ranches or a major centre, enabled women to earn an income from their efforts in the barnyard. At the turn of the century the Bateman and Copithorne families, both living in the Jumping Pound district west of Calgary, took advantage of their location near the booming city to supplement their ranching income with cream sales. In both families, women were the driving force behind their dairy production. The Batemans' cows were milked out in an open corral, even in inclement weather, with Mrs. Bateman doing the bulk of the work, for she "was a good milker and could milk two cows to anyone else's one."[30] Susan Copithorne, whose family became one of the most well-established ranching families in the Jumping Pound area, had come to Canada from Ireland as a child's maid and then married a pioneer rancher. Her family recalled her devotion to the life to which she had committed and explained how her efforts contributed to the family's success, despite its humble beginnings. Undaunted by the inevitable hard work and isolation that accompanied her lifestyle, "Susan saw no sense in wallowing in self-pity. She had chosen to be a settler's wife and was determined to make the best of it. She learned to milk cows and churn butter. She raised chickens and traded butter and eggs at the IG Baker store in Calgary. Where else would the groceries come from, the bolts of calico and denim?"[31] Her contributions directly supported the development of the Copithornes' ranch. From their start in a log cabin with a sod roof they gradually acquired enough land and their mixed-farm operation evolved into a profitable Hereford beef outfit. As the family recalled, from their subsistence beginning, based largely on dairy, they reached the point where "Holstein [a milk cow] was a dirty word."[32] Like the Copithornes, many families not only consumed the food that women produced in the barnyard, but used it as a means of earning cash to maintain their standard of living while income from primary production was reinvested in the operation for growth, enabling the expansion and development of the ranch.

As well as supplementing the family's income by their efforts in the barnyard, women grew gardens, raised poultry and hogs, and milked dairy cattle for the family's subsistence needs. By providing the family with sustenance they had grown and prepared, women averted the need for major expenditures on groceries. Food production was one of the most fundamental ways to save money on a frontier where provisions were not only hard to access but expensive. In many early communities the provisions available for purchase were minimal, and because the majority of ranches were located at some distance from towns, most families made only occasional and well-planned trips for supplies. The Porter family, for example, who ranched in southern Alberta in the early 1900s, had to make a sixty-five-mile, two-day trip to town for groceries.[33] As late as the 1920s, the "grub stake" (the provisions and groceries) for the Rocking P Ranch was only picked up once a month.[34] Women's labour in providing home-grown food was not only an economic advantage, but a necessity; fresh goods were simply not available for purchase. Bought supplies typically included staples such as flour, cornmeal, sugar, salt, coffee, dried fruit, and raisins.[35] Home-raised meat, also a staple, was kept frozen when possible or put up in salt brine. Chickens were challenging to raise when ranch infrastructure was primitive, as Eliza May attested when she recalled that during her first winter on the range, in 1889, most of her chickens "were frozen stiff as [they] only had a small log stable for them."[36] Even so, hens were a fixture of virtually every yard and were a much appreciated food source. Maxine and Dorothy Macleay wrote enthusiastically about the meat and eggs their flock provided during the winter of 1925: "Max and her 'pard' plucked eleven chickens on Jan 25th 1925. . . . Egg production has increased this month. The first of February was celebrated by everyone having fresh eggs for breakfast."[37]

When domestically raised meat was unavailable, many families turned to hunting and fishing. Women who were comfortable with a gun and an accurate shot were a valuable asset on the family ranch. Shooting for security, hunting, or sport was common among both men and women. Thanks to a longtime British fondness for gaming, many immigrant women, particularly from the upper classes, were proficient with a rifle. They found the wilderness of the West ideal for hunting, both for sport and for provisioning their pantries. Evelyn Cameron, whose husband managed the CC Ranch along Mosquito Creek, was a practiced shot and rarely rode

2.4 Edith and Fred Ings shooting gophers at the Midway Ranch (c.1911–12). Courtesy of Loree family.

out without packing a gun. She regularly shot prairie chicken and ducks and also used her gun to protect the poultry house. One of her letters expressed her remorse at having mistakenly shot a muskrat: "I shot a musk-rat one day, it too [like a previous skunk] was eating the dog's meat. I was very sorry afterwards. I thought it was a mountain cat and would eat the chickens, but musk-rats are quite harmless, and pretty creatures."[38]

Some women who hadn't come west with firearms skills learned to shoot out of the necessity of providing food for their families. Mary Alice Halton, who arrived with her large family to the Pincher Creek area in 1902, quickly "became a crack shot and kept the larder stocked with prairie chickens, Hungarian partridge and ducks."[39] Fishing was her specialty and the creek was well stocked with trout: "she often rode down on horseback to fill a sack with fish – occasionally even casting from astride her horse."[40] Near Priddis, Monica Hopkins wrote of the fresh trout she caught while ice fishing in January as providing a "welcome change" to her family's diet, even though her pantry was well stocked with frozen meat:[41]

> We have hanging in the storehouse a side of beef and one pork, a number of partridge and prairie chicken, and about a dozen roosters. My heart sinks every time I go into the storehouse because whatever I choose has to be thawed out before I can cook it and the meat has to be sawed up into joints. It is all frozen solid and takes at least two days to thaw out and I'm always forgetting to get something in until we are down to the very tag end. It's at times like that that the fish come in handy.[42]

In some homes, wild game provided some much appreciated variety to a repetitive diet, while in other homes it was a necessary staple. Whatever their means or their reasons, women became familiar with the western landscape and wildlife in order to provide for their families.

Homegrown vegetables, eaten fresh in season and canned or stored for the winter months, were an important part of the pioneer diet. The work of establishing, maintaining, and harvesting a vegetable garden was laborious, intensive, and essential. The largest ranches employed full-time gardeners, but on most family ranches it was the resident women who did the majority of the gardening. Women of all stations and on all sizes of ranches tended gardens. When Evelyn Cochrane arrived at their CC

2.5 Alice Gardiner working in the garden on Wineglass Ranch (c.1907–08). Reproduced with permission of Glenbow Archives.

Ranch from England every spring, one of her immediate tasks was to prepare the gardens for planting. Her diary attests to the continuous seasonal work, the challenge of gardening on the northern plains, and women's role in providing provisions for their family while assisting with ranch work and caring for the children. Two days after her arrival on the ranch in May 1904, Cochrane began gardening. On May 9, the sweet peas were put in the ground; three days later, she planted the rest of the seeds in the "hot-bed."[43] What followed was a repetitive cycle of weeding and watering, which on some outfits entailed hauling water from a considerable distance. Due to the elevation and northern climate, women soon learned that the growing season in Alberta is short and thus intensive. In 1904 the gardening season was finished by mid-September, but Cochrane, like other women, continued to provide for her family: "September 13th hard frost 10 [degrees] the garden, flowers and potatoes are killed. Very cold wind – branded 45 calves. Boy's face and hands sore and swelled kept him in the house." Two weeks later she wrote: "Boy almost well. I drove with him to Nanton for beef and oats. Shot some chicken and duck on the way."[44]

Though the garden was typically a woman's domain, husband and wife teams often shared the burden of work that was necessary for their common benefit. Neth argues that on family operations, "despite ideological separations between 'masculine' and 'feminine' work, the reality of the family labour system often prevented such clear demarcations in the actual performance of work."[45] Though many women – like Evelyn Springett, who did the back-breaking work of establishing her yard and garden herself – relished the time spent in their gardens and the reward of flowers and food, others, such as Monica Hopkins, failed to find enjoyment in having their hands in the dirt. For them, the garden was simply another aspect of their work. While some women wrote glowingly about their gardens, often a major source of pleasure and pride on the prairie, Hopkins wrote that "gardening is quite new to me. I never did any at home, never even had the slightest inclination to do so, though I enjoyed the results of someone else's efforts. Now I am learning that it is quite hard work and I still fail to see where there is much pleasure in it."[46] Fortunately, her husband willingly assisted with the work in their garden, which was established in the shelter of a poplar grove about a mile from the house; the Hopkinses' garden was the product of their combined labours, and his expertise compensated for her inexperience.[47] In the spring they rode their horses to the garden armed with tools and seeds and at harvest time carried sacks of vegetables back to the house behind their saddles. Together they developed an efficient way to plant potatoes: "Billie ploughs a furrow and I come along and drop a 'spud' in every so often, then Billie ploughs another furrow and that covers them up."[48] With her husband at her side, the necessary task became more tolerable and Hopkins even had time to appreciate "the magnificent view" from their hilltop garden.[49]

In addition to taking responsibility for the barnyard chores that sustained their families, the day-to-day activity of ranch women consisted largely of domestic work within the home, cooking, cleaning, and caring for children. The demands of maintaining a home and providing sustenance for hardworking and often rapidly expanding families meant that women's work was unremitting. However, women and girls who worked on the range and in ranch houses were not simply subservient drudges, as has so often been claimed by historians analyzing pioneer agriculture.[50] Ranch women's personal and published writings reflect that, despite their staggering workload and the lack of household conveniences, many found their work empowering and invigorating. The published words of women speak glowingly about the freedom and egalitarianism afforded by the ranching frontier. In an early article meant to depict the reality of a woman's daily routines on the ranch, Agnes Skrine of the Bar S, writing as Moira O'Neil, stated, "I am not concerned to prove that there is no life more enviable than this which we lead. I may think so, or I may not. But I am concerned to show that a lady's life on a ranch – that it consists necessarily and entirely of self-sacrifice and manual labour – is delusional."[51] As part of a literary trend that popularized women's writing from the West in the first decades of the twentieth century, women's depictions of the work they did in their homes and on the range reinforced the notion that the West afforded autonomy for all. According to historian Dee Garceau, the genre of "women's homesteading narratives" coincided with the emerging concept of New Womanhood that idealized an independent woman.[52] Placed in the context of the 1900s through the 1920s, these published works illuminate how women perceived themselves in the ranchers' West and in relation to changes in gender roles occurring in society at large; "by the second decade of the twentieth century, the separate spheres of Victorian society had blurred, and conventional wisdom urged women toward developing personal autonomy in a heterosocial world. . . . [H]omesteading [or ranching] became a compelling metaphor for female transformation."[53] Whatever the degree to which they glorified women's day-to-day work, published narratives and memoirs depicted the ranching frontier as a space where women genuinely relished the opportunity to create a home and a lifestyle that sustained their families and still left room for personal fulfilment.

Ranch women worked out of necessity and obligation, but also out of a desire for the adventure and opportunity connected with the early ranching industry. The frontier provided women with the challenge of managing and tending to their *own* homes, an experience that women from the upper classes found liberating and one that women from the lower classes found empowering. In her published memoirs, Montana rancher Isabel Randall wrote that she embraced the work she undertook on the frontier. Raised in a British home that had been maintained by servants, in the West she maintained the household, took care of a barnyard full of animals, and helped with the ranch work:

> I do think that this is the best sort of life. One feels so much better and happier; and so would any other healthy girl. Of course, washing dishes, scrubbing floors, and all the rest of it, does seem a great hardship to people at home; but I assure you it doesn't seem so when you do it. I know I would not exchange my happy, free, busy, healthy life out here, for the weariness and *ennui* that makes so many girls at home miserable.[54]

The size and condition of her home affected the amount of work a ranch woman had to do, yet class was a factor that mattered little in the daily realities of sustaining a home and family on the frontier. Women in one- or two-room shacks had different challenges and needs than more privileged women, such as Edith Ings, who had come west to live in a fully furnished two-story sandstone house complete with a maid's staircase, or Elizabeth Lane, who wrote that her home on the Flying E Ranch was "the largest log house I had ever known."[55] However, the tasks associated with maintaining a ranch and home erased many of the markers of class division based on labour and occupation. Because it was difficult to employ – or, more specifically, to hold on to – household staff, women in all socioeconomic groups had to adapt to managing their homes and performing menial domestic and barnyard work. Even women from the moneyed upper-middle class had to learn to be resourceful cooks and housekeepers and to tend the barnyard animals. Most found the process liberating, even if somewhat frustrating at first. According to the travel memoirs of the Duchess of Somerset, her friend Lady Adela Cochrane, a part owner in the Little Bow Cattle Company who also owned land and a lumber business, learned to raise chickens and keep milk cows. Somerset described the difficulty that the two women had in handling the semi-feral chicken: "Adela's sitting hens require a lot of running after; half wild, and as fleet as hares . . . so we have to get some of the men to help us run them down."[56] Randall, too, quickly and competently adapted to a wide range of practical work. Upon dismissing her servant, she successfully devised an efficient method of mopping the floor by making a mop out of an old broom handle and a worn shirt; learned the best ways to thaw frozen bread dough; and handled a wide range of jobs outdoors, such as gentling horses, driving the hay rake, and caring for a hundred hogs. In one of her letters, Randall nonchalantly remarked that though "the ground is *paved* with pigs . . . they don't bother me, as I always greet them with boiling water when they come round the kitchen door."[57] Indeed, published writings by women suggest that they relished the diversity and challenges associated with frontier domesticity and handled their demanding workload with fortitude.

As historian Lewis Thomas notes, "the actual work the women of the ranches had to do was very much the same as that of housewives everywhere who are without servants."[58] In general, women were primarily responsible for the upkeep of their homes and the care of their children. However, this did not relegate them to the confines of the home, as Thomas suggests in his comment that "ranch women rarely did much outdoor work. . . . [O]n many ranches very little of the work which on farms is traditionally done by women was done at all."[59] Ranching women's sense of space and place extended to encompass the barnyard and the range beyond the fences. While this study is not a comparative one, much of my research suggests that ranch women seem to have understood a more expansive sense of space and responsibility than their farming counterparts. Women were included in the sense of adventure that accompanied running large herds of cattle and horses, and many female ranchers, like the cowboys, held a romanticized appreciation of the landscape and their occupation.

Descriptions of early ranch women routinely associated them with elements of the working ranch. The Rowe sisters, for instance, ranched with their father near Pincher Creek after the death of their mother in 1909: Dorothy was "the lover of all horses and loved to ride," while "green grass and cattle have always been an important part of Gladys' life."[60] Evidence clearly indicates that the outdoor work of women and children was important on ranches of all sizes during the earliest frontier days and has remained so into the subsequent generations.

Women and children were the resident "cowboys" on family-run livestock operations. Compared to the open-range ranches that depended on the skills of hired cowboys, most family ranches operated with minimal hired help. When possible, a hired man was employed to provide additional labour, particularly for seasonal work, but even then, families worked directly alongside their help. George Zarn worked as a hired hand for several ranches in the foothills west of Stavely and Nanton and noted the distinction between working for a family operation and for a large-scale outfit: "It was different working on smaller ranches than big ones like the Bar U or Rod Macleay's where they had steady riders. On the small ranches on Willow Creek everyone was a rider when there were cattle to be moved, branded, etc."[61] This shortage of employed "man-power" necessitated women's direct involvement in the work of the ranch at large. Despite Zarn's accurate assessment that smaller ranches were more likely to use the help of women and children than were the larger operations, even the substantial Rocking P Ranch owned by Macleay used the work of female family members. As part of the curriculum designed by their governess, Macleay's daughters Dorothy and Maxine created a magazine called the *Rocking P Gazette* that, among other things, documented the daily events of the ranch. Few sources so clearly and explicitly detail ranch life from a female perspective; fully illustrated, this invaluable source indicates that these girls were an integral part of the working operation.

Dorothy and Maxine were on familiar terms with the cowboys, who considered the girls to be highly productive members of the crew. The hired hands admired the sisters and contributed humorous and eulogistic poems about their exploits to the *Gazette*, including this one:

See the feminine Cow-boy
As she rides the meadows through
Swings her quirt with careless joy,
While dashing off the dew . . .
They would rather be out riding
For the Boss of the Anchor P
And on the snow be sliding
Than play golf with their Aun-tee.[62]

Countless entries in the *Gazette* document the work performed by Dorothy and Maxine alongside the ranch hands and their father, whom they referred to as "Boss." For instance, a 1924 issue notes that "Jan 30th was a very hard day for Clem, Max, and her 'pard.' They worked swift and fast at the Calf Camp separating the fat calves from the beef calves."[63] Several months later, it was written that "Bert Beacook helped by Max and her 'pard' moved 215 head of steers from Section 33 to the Mountain field Sept. 23."[64] Another issue relates that the "home field [was] worked by the Boss, Max and her 'pard.' on Feb 19th. Fifty-six head were cut and then taken over to the Bar S feed ground."[65] The Macleay girls were also a productive unit when they rode out together on their own, supplementing the work done by the hired cowboys: "Max and her pard rode the west field and found 24 more calves that were missed when the field was rounded up earlier in the month" was a typical entry appearing in the *Gazette*.[66]

The size of the Rocking P Ranch necessitated hired help, yet these girls were not relegated to the home; rather, they were members of a large team that worked collectively to tend the stock. Equally comfortable in the saddle or in the barnyard – where they plucked chickens, milked wild cows, and planted potatoes – the sisters were experienced in all facets of the ranch's management and fully prepared to take over when they inherited it from their father after his death in 1953.[67] As a result of their upbringing on a ranch that functioned as a "family enterprise," historian Henry Klassen explains, "Dorothy and Maxine became the owners of the Rocking P

2.6 Not all milk cows were docile. Here, one of the Macleay girls is captured in cartoon form helping to milk a wild cow (1924). *Rocking P Gazette*, courtesy of Clay Chattaway.

and the Bar S Ranches respectively and they managed their ranches with the same diligence and prudent care their father had exercised in his business."[68]

On ranches of every size, from the 1880s through to the present, women have been directly responsible for overseeing the cattle stocking the range. It is this facet of ranch women's experience that has been most obscured by the myth of a cattlemen's fraternity dominated by hardworking cowboys and cattle kings. Rarely are women's roles on the range documented so cogently and descriptively as in the *Rocking P Gazette*; nonetheless, it is impossible to ignore the fact that women did a significant amount of the stock work on many ranches. Even in the 1880s and 1890s, when gender roles were most proscriptive, women in the West were afforded a freedom created by the absence of established society and frequently accompanied their partners or rode out alone.[69] As more family ranches were established at the turn of the twentieth century and during the decades that followed, it became increasingly apparent that women's labour was required to help manage and tend to stock, both in the barnyard and on the range.[70] Many of the jobs had to be done on horseback. Some of the cattle work was seasonal and performed universally on all ranches, like gathering and sorting for branding, weaning, and fall roundups; additionally, each ranch had its own particular patterns of pasture rotation and herd management that demanded almost daily riding. "Feminine cowboys" made it possible for families to keep up with the seasonal work and the day-to-day operations.[71] Some women did more than assist with the cattle work, assuming full responsibility for managing their families' herds. One of these women was Doris Burton, whose memoirs descriptively illustrate the nature of work performed by ranching women, be it roping, branding, or, in this case, sorting cattle on her own while her husband was away on the rodeo circuit:

> One big chore was to gather the open heifers, thirty four head, out of the big herd before the bulls went out. The gate to cut them back through was situated in the worst of all places to get very reluctant animals through. It had a deep, steep narrow coulee fifty yards from the cutting-out gate. To accomplish that job was a hard battle between a good horse and a dodging, hard running heifer. . . . It took a sure-footed horse to race down and up, or up and down in that wicked coulee and to not trip or fall on the run. I did that chore for years and didn't like that coulee or gate any better the first time or the last. I only had one horse fall once due to the wetness of the earth.[72]

While many ranch women relished the adventure and opportunity that accompanied the increased scope of their responsibilities, outdoor work was not without its challenges. Though ranch women were typically undaunted by physical labour and rarely complained in writing about inclement weather or other hardships, their concern for their children's well-being while they were performing their endless chores appears to be one of the most ubiquitously stressful aspects of ranching. A woman's particular stage of life considerably affected the amount of work she had to do and how she perceived her experience. Single women or women with grown children typically had a reduced domestic workload and more freedom to enjoy their time out of the home than those caring for young families. With livestock to tend to in all sorts of conditions, women used creative strategies both in caring for their children and in carrying out the ranch work. In her memoirs, Catherine Neil recalled the infamously frigid winter of 1906–07, when she and her sister-in-law were required to help the men feed the starving stock: "Each morning after tucking in my baby to keep her warm, my sister-in-law and I each carried a bundle of hay on our backs and threw it out by the handful, so that the sheep would follow, while the men went ahead with a snow plough, trying to cut the snow down to the grass."[73] As families grew, leaving the children unattended became increasingly worrisome for women who had to work out of the house. Neil recalled another trying winter where she worked alongside her husband to feed the stock: "When winter came I had to drive the sleigh with the hay, while my husband forked it out. My little children, three of them now, had to be left in the house all alone, and many a time my heart was in my mouth, as the saying goes, wondering if they were touching the fires."[74]

Expanding the breadth of a woman's sphere into the barnyard and beyond offered a diversity of and opportunity for new experiences, but leaving the house unattended for any length of time compounded the amount of work to be done upon her return. While many women spoke of the satisfaction of caring for their homes and children and the fulfilment of outdoor work, others, like Nellie Hutchison-Taylor, wrote candidly about trying to uphold this balance:

> If I went out for more than a few minutes I would come back to find the fire out, children squalling, dishes to be washed, no hot water, and dinner to get. Sometimes I longed to fly away to some place where there would be no stoves to burn my fingers, no scrubbing to be done to harden my hands and fill my nails with slivers, no cooking – but that would pass off and I would go at it again.[75]

The delicate balance of family obligation, economic investment, and personal fulfilment kept ranch women engaged and content in their duties. If the balance in any of these areas shifted, such as in the absence of a supportive partner or during times of economic stress, the challenge of caring for dependent livestock and children put extraordinary demands on women's time and personal resources.

Many variables affected women's day-to-day obligations and the contributions they made to their households. Thus, how they perceived the burdens they bore differed greatly according to individual circumstances. The refreshingly honest diary of Nellie Hutchison-Taylor illustrates how personal conditions, perhaps even more so than external factors such as class and environment, affected the quality of life for pioneer ranch women. As much as pioneers wanted to believe the propaganda that the West promised everyone a chance for reinvention and opportunity, in reality pioneers needed to possess practical skills and practice prudent financial management in order to succeed. Nellie and her husband lacked both of these traits when, having made some unfortunate "speculations in the Old Country," they immigrated to Canada, "the Land of Promise," in 1884.[76] After two years in Quebec they optimistically ventured to the West, at first squatting and then eventually acquiring a 160-acre homestead and 160-acre preemption on land west of Calgary when the Cochrane Lease was opened to settlers. With the establishment of their frontier home, Hutchison-Taylor recalled, her "trials and tribulations" began.[77] She discovered that maintaining a home under primitive conditions with little income was a daunting and unforgiving job: "I thought I knew a little of the hardship of life, but I soon discovered what a helpless, useless creature I was. . . . [W]e had frittered our money away and had no income except what we earned."[78] After a succession of failures, attributable to their lack of agricultural experience and to drought, the couple moved 130 miles north of Calgary. This time the collapse of their trading business and the death of her husband led Hutchison-Taylor to take over the management of their livestock and new homestead. She remarried several years later, and financial troubles continued to plague her because, as she recounted, "neither of us were very saving and my husband kept open house for his friends. It all takes money and the debts began to accumulate and we could see no hope of getting clear."[79] She eventually sold her remaining stock and moved to Calgary to live with her children until a doctor's orders sent her back to the better air found "pioneering near the foothills."[80] Hutchison-Taylor's honest portrayal of repeated failures on the frontier serves as an illustrative comparative analysis to more positive depictions of pioneer experience. The same personal qualities, such as a willingness to enter into unknown ventures and the belief in the inherent opportunity of the West, led some to success while others, without the advantages of practical experience or necessary business sense, became caught up in the perpetual cycle of searching for the next "promised land."

Measuring a woman's or a ranch's "success" is a highly subjective task. Even though in her own analysis, Hutchison-Taylor perceived her pioneering experience to be a failure, to some extent the very presence of her story in a local history book – surrounded by accounts of brave entrepreneurial men, selfless women, and ranching and farming families that have now been on the land for generations – can be seen as an accomplishment in itself. She led a hardworking life, and her honesty about her struggle to maintain the balance between family and finances on the ranching frontier is a valuable contribution to our understanding of women's pioneer experience and how the vagaries of the beef industry affected real people. Other women left more tangible legacies and their efforts are more commonly defined as successful; their ranches had provided them and their immediate families with a livelihood, and they left the gift of good land to their children, who continued to ranch for generations. One would guess that this is what most women desired when they embarked, willingly or unwillingly, on their journey to the cattle frontier.

As this chapter has illustrated, through women's day-to-day contributions the family ranch became the mainstay in the beef economy of Alberta. The role of women in this process was especially apparent during exceptional circumstances. For the duration of World War I, when many eligible men enlisted and served overseas, women's efforts kept ranches operational. Their ability to manage varied tasks and responsibilities enabled ranching families to stay on the land. For women accustomed to working alongside their partners, the physical jobs of managing livestock and putting up crops remained largely the same. A significant change for them was an increase in their influence over the management of ranch business. In the absence of their husbands and sons, women's responsibilities extended to include directly overseeing hired help, marketing cattle and horses, and making the critical decisions on their own. Just as women in society at large became increasingly emancipated as a result of being thrust into the public workforce as part of the war effort, ranch women became progressively empowered by their new positions of authority within the cattle industry. Some used this opportunity to develop and assert their business acumen, as in the case of Josephene Bedingfeld, who was already recognized as an accomplished horsewoman.[81] With women's elevated position of power, some found it challenging after the war ended to make the transition back to working with their spouses. Sarah Gardner, whose husband had left on the very day he heard of the outbreak of war and was absent for four years, proved herself capable as ranch manager of their large outfit in the foothills. When her husband returned to Alberta, they had to renegotiate their division of labour and authority.[82] The necessity of maintaining agricultural production on the home front during World War I emphasized women's importance on family ranches and in the cattle industry as a whole.

Just as they had sustained family ranches during the war, women often drew on their resourcefulness to provide the stability and ingenuity needed for a ranch to remain viable in times of particular economic hardship. The Depression years of the 1930s, which brought financial stressors as well as unprecedented drought to the prairies, were especially hard for families dependent on small commercial beef herds. George Zarn, who had worked for several families struggling to keep their ranches afloat during those years, commented sardonically that "the Brazil ranch was like all ranches that didn't have a brewery behind them in the thirties. They all owned a big mortgage."[83] The financial stress caused by big debts, little income, and a compounding drought that saw crops fail and livestock suffer added tensions to many domestic situations. In some cases, women found themselves in a position to not only run their ranches, but pull them back from the brink of financial ruin. During the thirties, Elsie Gordon resolved to hold on to her ranch and home despite the odds. Her father and mentor, George Lane, had died several years earlier "with very little but a memory left," despite his many years as a major player in the Alberta cattle industry.[84] Then her husband deserted her and their three young children, having decided that "the dirty thirties were too much for a person to eke out a living from the land"; he disappeared one afternoon after saying he was going to town for parts.[85] Nonetheless, Mrs. Gordon was deeply rooted in the land and able to manage her remaining assets creatively in order to hold on to the ranch. As her children later recalled, in a memorial letter written to their mother,

> You had the creek and the Oxley in your blood and you knew one way or another you could support and educate your family by staying on the ranch. By going through Farm Credit, a very

> demoralizing experience, you were able to carry on, paying off a mortgage you had inherited when you purchased the ranch.[86]

Gordon not only "carried on," but, equipped with the practical skills she had acquired throughout her life, she drove, did the mechanical work on her own vehicles, rode and did cattle work in a side saddle, gardened and grew acres of corn, donated land for a schoolhouse, earned the respect and admiration of her neighbours, and managed a successful ranch that was passed on to her children and is now operated by her granddaughter Jennifer Barr.[87]

Like Elsie Gordon, Edith Ings was left with a big mortgage and a ranch to run when her husband, Fred Ings, died at the height of the Depression in 1936. Having already sold off her beloved Sunset Ranch, she was determined to maintain the holdings of the homeplace, the Midway Ranch, and her summer home and grazing land, Trail's End. Combining her ranching experience with innovative entrepreneurship, she continued to ranch with the help of her daughters Mary and Constance and supplemented their income by opening their summer headquarters in the Porcupine Hills as Trail's End Riding Camp. In doing so, Mrs. Ings capitalized on the growing trend of "western" holidays on dude ranches, offering her guests trail rides, serene surroundings, and the chance to see a functional working ranch that was managed, at the time, by women.[88] The additional income provided by the dude ranch enabled the cattle operation to stay afloat during the late 1930s and to continue successfully into the next decade. During World War II the guest ranch flourished particularly by hosting young Commonwealth air force pilots who were on their leave from training at southern Alberta airbases. Edith Ings's strategy for saving the ranch was successful. By the time she died, Ings had sustained a legacy that was passed on to her daughters. Constance and her husband, William Loree, continued to ranch, and both remained on the land until their deaths. The Midway Ranch and Trail's End remain in the family and are currently ranched by its third, fourth, and fifth generations.

Even as early as the turn of the nineteenth century the economic premise of ranching was well established. As L. V. Kelly remarked in 1913, "no business in the world can recuperate from the losses that the cattle industry receives and recovers from."[89] Ranching was, and continues to be, a relatively low-income and labour-intensive business; however, because of the vested interest and labour of family members, the family ranch has endured. On the western frontier where the presence of a woman was initially so uncommon that milk cows balked, horses spooked, and puppies fled at the sight of one, women became eagerly and actively engaged in establishing economically diversified family ranches.[90] Women's labour has been fundamental in the process of sustaining small and mid-size ranches through unprofitable periods and maintaining the operation without having to hire profit-destroying outside labour. The same factors that distinguished them from the large corporate spreads, such as close management and labour-intensive subsistence work in the barnyard, were what made family input so critical to the success of smaller ranches. Women devoted their full energies to the success of the family ranch, ensuring that ranches were able not only to survive, but to thrive and be passed along. By participating in the primary economic production of early ranches and providing their families with support and sustenance, women enabled the longevity of the family ranch, while at the same time dismantling barriers of gender-specific labour, proving that women adapted to the conditions of the frontier as well as their male counterparts. The creation of the family ranch afforded women the opportunity to create and sustain something concrete and enduring, a lifestyle and a livelihood particular to the northwestern cattle ranges.

CHAPTER THREE

Gender Roles and Working Partnerships on the Ranch

More than mere "helpmates," ranching women on family operations were, as demonstrated in the previous chapter, directly engaged with the productive labour of their ranches and provided invaluable domestic labour that supplemented the ranch's primary income and sustained their families within the home. Sharing responsibilities in a working partnership not only helped make the family ranch an enduring form of agriculture, but also led to a negotiated sense of gender relations and a restructuring of the historically hierarchical order of labour roles for all family members. This chapter examines how existing divisions of labour were transformed and gender roles blurred by the realities of ranch work, addresses how women's status within their personal relationships remained complicated by the patriarchal roots of agriculture, and demonstrates that in the presence of mutuality and shared decision making the conditions of the ranching frontier made the ideals of companionate marriage possible.

Early ranchers came to the West accompanied by their cultural mores and their perceptions of gender appropriateness. The ideological boundaries distinguishing the socially constructed female private sphere of the home and the masculine public sphere of productive labour in urban Victorian and Edwardian society were present on the frontier, but not rigid or impermeable. Some men (and women) subscribed to the views that historian Lewis Thomas described in his early analyses of Albertan ranching communities. Thomas suggested that "the English tradition was strong enough to make it difficult for men to believe that the woman who was too weak to pass a tea-cup in the dining-room was strong enough to milk a cow in the stable."[1] However, my research into the working practices of ranching families reveals that this proscriptive gender bias was not universal. From as early as the 1880s, women were accepted as a valued part of the working family ranch. Even on ranches that employed both domestic servants and hired men, such as the Midway Ranch established in 1903, women were both expected and self-motivated to help with primary production and subsistence work.[2] Similarly, in her study of the historic and modern roles of Texas ranch women, Elizabeth Maret challenges typical analyses of the gendered division of labour roles with very real evidence that women have always played a role in the primary production of cattle operations. She writes: "ironically, the 'traditional' view of women's roles is predominantly from an urban-industrial perspective, which presumes separate spheres of activity for women and men. This traditional view of women is that of domestic specialist and helpmate to men. Men are defined and perceived as the economic providers and producers."[3] Working on ranches on cattle frontiers was, for many women raised in urban centres, their first opportunity to truly test these proscribed boundaries. And many men – again, for the first time – found themselves truly dependent on the direct and often physical support and labour of the women in their lives. Confining women's work to the insular sphere of the home was simply not the practical rural reality. As a result of the essential role that women played both within and outside the home, traditionally gendered hierarchies and gender specific labour roles gradually became less defined on most ranches. Men's and women's work was not always clearly demarcated into separate realms; the barnyard became the arena where labour and gender roles blurred and interconnected, and the range became the site where barriers of gender division were dismantled. For ranch women, a sense of home, work, and place encompassed an expansive space that extended beyond their domestic duties within the home to include the barnyard and the rangeland beyond.

The spatial dynamics and the nature of work on the family ranch during the development years of the late 1800s and early 1900s especially blurred the boundaries between gender-specific spheres of activity. A dual economy operated on the range. Scholar Jeanne Kay defines this model as "a subsistence or secondary economy that functions within the commercial staple export economy."[4] The lingering Victorian ideal of separate spheres was part of the cultural baggage that ranchers had brought with them from the East, but like many of the values brought west, it failed to transplant successfully and became modified by the conditions of the frontier. In theory, men's and women's labour roles were segregated into gender-specific spheres where the domestic, labour-intensive, and typically subsistence economy was deemed a private feminine sphere and the extensive production of staples, such as beef, for a commercial economy was deemed a public and masculine realm. High status and power through control of the primary cash income traditionally accompanied the masculine sphere. Feminists criticize this "doctrine of spheres" and the dichotomous power structure it creates as legitimizing a limiting view of women's activities and potentials. For in actuality, "the two economies swing in and out of balance with one another," alternately taking turns providing for and supporting the family and the business operation as financial conditions necessitate.[5] This balancing or blending of economic and domestic spheres was made evident by both the geography and the workloads that men and women had to navigate as they established their homes and ranches. The expansiveness of the landscape, the miles of unbroken and unfenced range that women and men negotiated so as to tend their herds, and the intensive and repetitive work involved in keeping the home meant that members of both sexes were necessarily engaged in the productive economy and the "secondary" domestic labour. In analyzing the working environment of the cattle frontier it is, as Kay notes, "defensible to view domestic and commercial spheres as useful economic and spatial abstractions independent of gender, and then to see how men and women moved between them."[6] On a family ranch the working environment included the home, the barnyard, and the range, with all members of the family functioning as necessary in all of these domains; physically and theoretically, women and men operated within the same framework on the frontier.

Though the official census record acknowledged only one "'main operator' on family-owned agricultural enterprises" – and "further assumes that this operator is a man unless there is no adult male present" – the unofficial record composed of memoirs, diaries, and photographs reveals that women worked directly alongside their partners or were indeed the "main operators" of their family ranches.[7] Women on ranches were, and

3.1 Constance Loree handling the branding irons at the fire (c.1940). Courtesy of Loree Family.

continue to be, directly involved in the primary production of raising beef cattle. Out of necessity and desire, women occupied labour roles that were typically held only by men in more established regions: they cared for livestock, assisted with any farming work, built fences and erected outbuildings, and rode the range. Women and girls were not only valuable assistants to husbands and fathers, but often acted as the primary producers and provided the impetus for enacting more rigorous management. In 1884, Mary Ella Inderwick commented on a neighbouring rancher in the Pincher Creek area. She wrote that "his wife is the leading spirit, and even goes out with him putting up fence because I suppose he would not go alone. She does the really hard labour."[8] Women's involvement in the work of managing and running their ranches enabled them to navigate and transcend traditional gender roles. Like the male ranchers, who both created and assimilated into the culture of the ranching frontier, women developed the skills, language, and familiarity with the environment that accompanied the work of raising beef cattle. In doing so, they experienced a kind of egalitarianism and independence that was not afforded them in more established communities in the East, where women's labour was typically either restricted to the uniquely female sphere of the home environment or committed to the constraints of paid employment. Ranch women were essentially self-employed. They took pride in their productivity while making tangible improvements and progress on their ranches and within their homes. The necessity of work moved women beyond the domestic sphere and began to integrate them into the mode of primary production. When there was work to be done, matters of propriety were subsumed by the reality of ranch life.

Standards of gender appropriateness were often ignored when there was vital work to be done; if women were required to assist the men with ranch work it became imperative for men, in turn, to help women with the burden of domestic chores. Of course, not every family blurred divisions of gendered labour, but many households regularly shared responsibility for some chores, like gardening and milking, that were typically considered women's work. Evidence indicates that not only did the cultural and physical environment of the West allow women to overcome the restrictions of late-Victorian constructions of gender, but the requirements of ranch life also afforded men the opportunity to experience life with fewer limitations on their behaviour. Even when attempting to adhere to cultural conventions that were transplanted onto the frontier, such as formal dinner parties, gender roles were subverted according to circumstance. After dining at a neighbouring ranch operated by a family of brothers and one sister, Inderwick reported that her hostess, Miss Smith, had "brought all her traditions with her."[9] Despite this, however, she wrote that "the dinner was very simple as they keep no cook, but do all the work themselves, and when we rose and swept from the room, we did not leave the men to enjoy a quiet smoke only, but to wash up. They appeared later looking guiltless of ever having seen a dish towel or dirty plate."[10] Men crossed the lines of traditionally separate gender roles to help their households, and ranches, run smoothly.

Men and women shared and balanced the workload according to what was practical at the time; in many cases that meant men helped with the domestic chores. In the late 1880s, Isabel Randall, her husband, and their friend Frank shared the burden of household duties, barnyard chores, and ranch work on their Montana outfit. Mrs. Randall wrote that "Jem, Frank and I are all pretty busy now, as we have all the domestic duties to perform."[11] She was a proficient rider and routinely did the horse or cattle work while one of the men cooked. In one particular instance, after riding all day to help sell horses to a visitor, she discovered that "when we got back, hungry and happy, about 7 o'clock, we found Frank had a regular banquet for us: bean soup, fresh-caught trout, haunch of venison with buffalo berry jelly, compote of (dried) apples, *and* a beautiful sponge cake, made with nothing but flour, water, sugar and eggs."[12] Even when chores were ordinarily segregated by sex, with women reigning in the kitchen, if a ranch wife was needed to help ride or do cattle work, it was possible that she would be assisted with the cooking or dishes upon her return. On their ranch in southwestern Saskatchewan, Lou Forsaith was primarily responsible for the home and children but also worked at all of the ranch jobs, which included feeding the cattle with her newborn daughter wrapped in a quilt and wedged between bales on the hayrack. Her husband was "quite willing" to come in and make supper and watch the children so that she could "go and do chores or something . . . get away from the house for a little while."[13] Monica and Billie Hopkins were equally flexible about labour roles on their Priddis horse ranch. As Monica was frequently needed to help with the riding, Billie made himself useful in the kitchen. One of Monica's lively letters illustrates that though each sex had its own particular area of responsibilities, the reality of balancing the duties of ranch and home meant that men and women crossed over and performed nontraditional duties that blurred the boundaries of gender-specific roles:

> My housekeeping is running fairly smoothly and I try to be systematic but what can you do when a husband dashes into the house as he did yesterday, and says, "Hurry up and get into your riding things, we are going to gather some horses and you had better come along too." I looked around the kitchen; the breakfast things weren't even washed up and I was just going to start the bread. I said, "I can't leave everything like this, and I have bread to start." Billie quickly put that objection aside by saying, "I'll make some baking powder biscuits when we get back; you go and get dressed and I'll put the things away."[14]

On the ranching frontier the presence of a man in the kitchen or with his hands in a washtub was only slightly less common than the sight of a woman riding out alone to check on stray stock or behind the lines of a hay mower. Of course, assessing the equitable nature of labour division is problematic and subjective at best. How does a historian account for the significant number of photographs from the frontier period depicting men at the washtub? In her shrewd "ficto-critical" rendering of the laborious task of laundry day, Aritha van Herk muses that "either those men have no woman to do the job for them, which is likely enough, or it was so amazing and unusual when they plunged their hands into a tub-full of water, someone just had to take a picture of them."[15] However, it is equally as likely that men simply took a proactive role to ensure that the work that had to be done was. This was the case for newlyweds Monica and Billie Hopkins; the clothes had to be washed and neither had the experience to do it. So they simply suffered together through the trial of learning to do laundry, often with hilarious results.[16] As Kay remarks, the realities of life in cattle country left room for "an expanded definition of the heroic male in the Old Wild West that includes domestic activities. . . . If the West was 'heaven for men and dogs' it was also a place where they cooked and cleaned for themselves, and sometimes for women as well."[17] On the frontier the home remained a women's realm, but men were welcomed into it and not emasculated by regularly performing domestic work.

3.2 Dave Blacklock doing his laundry (c.1913). Pioneer existence blurred the lines between traditionally gender-specific tasks. Reproduced with permission of Glenbow Archives.

Women's essential role in the productive labour of ranches and men's willingness to help with domestic duties did not automatically transfer into increased status for women and their work or necessarily indicate an egalitarian environment within the family. Complicated by factors such as primary male ownership of land and the overarching patriarchal power structures that had shaped political and familial values for centuries, women did not simply gain equality by performing "higher-prestige" men's work.[18] In fact, some historians, such as Canadian scholar Veronica Strong-Boag, have argued that as the barriers of gendered labour division were dismantled, pioneer women were further indentured by an increase in their workload.[19] Other causes deemed responsible for a rural woman's subjugation were the lack of modern conveniences, such as indoor plumbing, heating, and lighting; the improbability of labour-saving devices in the household; and her relative isolation with little reprieve from physical labour.[20] In practice, however, these factors did not affect a farm or ranch woman's quality of life nearly as much as did the nature of her relationship with her partner and the degree to which they shared responsibility for the management and day-to-day operations of their ranch. The limiting factors on female autonomy, which Dee Garceau suggests the New Woman of the twentieth century sought to overcome, were "family authority, domesticity, and female dependence."[21] As this book has thus far indicated, in many cases the frontier experience afforded women the chance to rise above these obstacles; however, when family life entailed unequal divisions of mobility, labour, and power, women then failed to experience the emancipation that so many others gained as a result of their ranching lifestyle.

One of the complexities of ranch women's experience was that the same factor that could increase their independence and resourcefulness could also make their lives more restrictive while also making men's domain more expansive. In many cases a woman's ability to maintain the yard, ranch, and home enabled a man to work out and earn much-needed income from external sources while the couple simultaneously "proved up" a homestead or established the foundations of their ranch. Often, however, this meant that women not only shouldered the bulk of the work, but had to endure the isolation that was compounded by their husband's prolonged absences. It was also the women's work on the home front that enabled their partners to play cowboy; in countless situations, women bore the burden of the daily responsibilities in the immediate vicinity of the home while men enjoyed the adventure of the range. Though some women were empowered by the personal fortitude it took to attend to ranch work in their husband's absence, many expressed frustration over the repetitive and isolating nature of their tasks. American historian Elliott West cites one Texas couple's binary depictions of their life on the range. When the Newcombs left their established life in town to start their own ranch, the patterns and rhythms of their once cohesive daily lives began to diverge. In his diary, Mr. Newcomb described his thrilling life on the range, "full of bluster and brag," as West notes.[22] His wife, however, wrote of an increasingly insular life: "a man that is cowhunting with a lively crowd has no idea how long and lonesome the time passes with his wife at home. . . . A man can see his friends, hear the news and pass time . . . , while his wife at home sees and hears nothing until he returns from a long trip tired and worn out."[23] An absent partner or one who simply "wasn't a helpmate" made the already arduous, and at times lonely, work of women all the more difficult.[24]

The work that brought many couples together was the same factor that caused discord and bitterness in other marriages. When workloads were unbalanced or when her partner shirked his responsibilities, unremitting work and isolation could make life enormously challenging for a ranch woman. Furthermore, when a marriage was founded on making a living off the land, and that land was legally owned by the male head of the household, women in abusive situations were in a position of extreme vulnerability. Factors such as scarce personal funds, isolation, a limited network of support, and their fundamental lack of legal property rights combined to keep women trapped in oppressive and abusive relationships.[25] While the nature of ranch work inspired equality in many partnerships, frontier conditions have been associated with an increase in domestic violence. The contradiction of women's vital roles on their ranches and their lack of power within domestic relationships is illustrated by the life of rancher Doris Burton. Ironically, behind her back Burton's husband credited her with keeping the ranch running, even though he was alternately abusive and dismissive. Reflecting on these incongruities, Doris Burton wrote:

> I long ago found that I was married to a man who expected me to take life's hard knocks on my own. He talked to other people as if he cared, but didn't let me know because it might make me a sissy! Imagine! It was through other rodeo cowboys' wives that I learned Ed replied to their questions of "How can you be rodeoing when you've got a big ranch to run?" Ed replied jokingly, "I've got a wife at home who can run the ranch better than I can." That was news to me, and I wished that I could do the muscular work as good as a man. I got things done, but it was harder on me than on a man, I'm sure.[26]

Knowing that he was dependent on her to keep the ranch operational, and that it was her greatest love, her husband continually threatened to sell the ranch at times when Burton was unable to come to her own defence – such as when she was in the hospital recovering from abdominal surgeries made necessary by overwork during her pregnancies. Burton was confident in her competence as a rancher, but vulnerable to the whims of an emotionally unstable husband and the patriarchal legal system that denied ranch and farm women ownership of the land they had worked and invested their lives into developing.[27] She sometimes justified his behaviour, attributing his cruelty to the stressors associated with establishing and running a ranch on meagre funds in the uncertain economic climate of the late 1920s. She wrote, for instance, "[Ed] was a slave driver and hard to please, but I understood the stress and tension and did my very best."[28] Her diligence, work ethic, amazing competence, and grace enabled her family to prosper even under the conditions of abuse she endured. Eventually, armed with the skill set and the self-confidence fostered by a lifetime of ranch work, Burton left her husband and forced him off the ranch that she had almost singlehandedly sustained. To circumvent the legal complexities associated with the divorce, the ranch was inherited by her granddaughters, but she continued to run it for them until her death.[29]

Ranch women had different motivators and used varied strategies to rise above adversity. Doris Burton was driven to overcome the hardships of her situation by an intrinsic love of the land, the animals, and the practice of ranching. For Mary Kropinak, who also endured overwork and an abusive and frequently absent husband, it was the determination to make a better life for her children that pushed her to continually advance against seemingly impossible circumstances. Unlike Burton, who had the constant companionship of her horses and dogs and the stimulation of having a significant ranch to run, Kropinak was isolated on a remote homestead in the foothills, with little food and a large family. Burton was personally committed to a lifetime of ranching, but Kropinak had reluctantly accompanied her husband to their homestead where he promised that having their own land and cattle would bring their family "security and freedom."[30] In actuality he had wanted a place that he could control, even if it was not large enough to support his family. A lifetime of overexertion caused Kropinak's early death, at the age of fifty-one, yet she lived to see three sons own land and livestock. At one point her son Frank held the prestigious position of "top rider" at the Walrond ranch. Kropinak's tenacity enabled her family to gradually expand their holdings from a meagre homestead shack and one milk cow to include a substantial and productive mixed hay and cattle ranch.[31] Subordination and unbalanced workloads were undoubtedly a part of the pioneer experience for some ranch women, but motivated by a desire for the lifestyle or a commitment to their family's well-being, women found ways to survive inequity and establish productive ranches that supported and sustained their souls and their families.

Even when inequity in a relationship or the vagaries of life gave them a heavy load to bear, ranch women performed work that connected them to the land in fulfilling and meaningful ways. In an interview, rancher and poet Rhoda Sivell recalled that she and her husband had mutually made the decision to emigrate in 1899 because "we wanted a free ranch life in the West."[32] She reflected on her experience: "Pioneering is a wonderful free life but I found out you have to pay for the life you love, and want, and stand up to all the hardships and storms in a strange land."[33] Burdened by her husband's ill health, with a large ranch to run in an arid and remote part of what is now eastern Alberta, Sivell independently managed their operation and yet still found the time to write the poetry that sustained her. First published in 1911, her poetry reflects the beauty of the place she came to call home and has an immediate, intimate resonance that indicates her familiarity with the land on which she lived and worked. One of her poems, "The Wood by the Saskatchewan," illustrates how the land she toiled in was both the source of, and a respite from, work:

> I came, when the dawn was breaking,
>
> To a wood by the river side,
>
> I rode from the far-off ranges
>
> Where the prairie stretches wide.
>
> Looking for stock that had wandered;
>
> Thinking they might have strayed
>
> Down to the wood by the river,
>
> So straight for the wood I made.
>
> I stayed in the wood by the river,
>
> The sun rose high on the plain,

And a voice from the range was calling
  Me back to my work again.
I forgot for a time my duty,
  For the place held joys for me,
And the peace I found by the river
  Set my weary spirit free.[34]

Like the tone that echoes in so much of ranch women's writing, the voice in Sivell's poetry is shaped by place and experience. She claimed for herself, and for all ranch women, a rightful and essential spot on the range. Ranch women were at home on the rangeland, and the comfortable connection they had with their working environment enabled them to do the jobs they had to do with grace and brought them relief from the weight of the work they performed.

In an extensive analysis of the social dynamics within family farms in the American Midwest, historian Mary Neth teases out the complexities of workload and power distribution. Modified, of course, by differences in time and place, her insights aptly apply to the family ranch as well. Neth concludes that in the presence of "mutuality," family agriculture was made both viable as a business endeavour and empowering as a lifestyle: "By emphasizing work flexibility, shared responsibilities, and mutual interests, farm people limited the conflicts created by the patriarchal structure of the family and agriculture and created strategies for the survival of family farms."[35] To argue either that the burden of work expected of women saddled them to lives of unrelenting drudgery and abuse or that the freedom of the frontier was entirely empowering negates the complexities of women's lived experience. Mutuality best describes the domestic and working relationships of most ranching families. Elliott West defines the "pioneer household" as "an economic mechanism of mutually-dependent parts"; in its totality, a frontier family was a "productive unit, often a remarkably effective and self-sustaining one."[36]

Distributing power equally within the family was one of the most effective ways in which ranchers kept family dynamics harmonious and made the ranch a viable economic unit. Involving women and children in the decision-making processes of a ranch ensured that the entire family was committed and personally invested in the well-being of the operation. Joan Lawrence, who saw her children and grandchildren flourish on their ranch near the Cypress Hills, wrote that "the best part of raising children on a ranch is their sharing in the work and the decision-making. I think that's wonderful."[37] There were practical reasons for including the whole family in the work and management of smaller ranches. When women were responsible for the cattle or the crops, it only made sense that they would also be a part of the decision making that went into their management. Every spring when her husband was busy in the fields, wrote Doris Fenton, "the cows were mine. . . . I had to sort out the cows and calves and put them out with the bulls. I had to dehorn the commercial calves and do horn weights and all that kind of thing. . . . When it came to making decisions, I always had my 'say so.' We didn't always do what I said, but very often we did."[38] By including even the youngest members of the household in the working details, families prepared for both the best and the worst possibilities: the expansion and succession of the ranch by the younger generation or incapacitating accidents or death. Vivian Bruneau Elli, whose family ranched in southern Saskatchewan, reflected that by including the entire family in decisions that affected their daily lives, her father had fostered a working environment that facilitated equality and independence. In addition, as she told a friend, her father had insisted that the ranch was run as a family affair: "He always wants us to know about everything. One of these days he could have an accident and he wants us to be able to make decisions and carry on."[39] Many family ranches were collaborative ventures that required the labour, knowledge, and commitment of the entire family, both inside the home and on the range. Each member of the family was made more effective and responsible when they were included in the decisions that affected the day-to-day operations of the ranch.

Women's contribution to the daily productive labour of ranches is undeniably evident on ranches of all sizes and within a multitude of family conditions, but their role in the management of operations is less definitive and more difficult to ascertain. Even within similar social classes and peer groups, women maintained various levels of engagement with the business operations of their ranches. The differing levels of involvement of the wives of two of the founders of the Calgary Stampede demonstrate the multiplicity of ranch women's experiences. Some women, like Elizabeth Lane, had little to do with ranch business. She deferred to the business decisions of her husband, George Lane, even though he had somewhat of an impulsive nature. He bought and sold land and livestock alongside the major players in the early cattle industry, but left little financial legacy behind after his death in 1925.[40] In her memoirs, "Mrs. George Lane" referred to ranching as her husband's "business."[41] All references to property acquisitions are mentioned as George's purchases; there is no indication of mutuality, even in regards to major investments like purchasing one of the largest intact ranches in southern Alberta. She wrote simply that "in 1904 George bought the Bar U Ranch."[42] She also projected herself as separate from their financial troubles, writing that "in 1907 it looked as though all the big cattlemen were broke, George Lane included, but the situation was saved with grim work and trying."[43] In comparison, Florence and Guy Weadick integrated all of their endeavours, from performing in Wild West shows to raising cattle to operating a dude ranch. According to rancher Lenore Maclean, who grew up next to the Weadicks' Stampede Ranch near Longview, Alberta, the influential and entrepreneurial Alberta couple "had a truly good partnership. He was an organizer and had a vision. She was a stable business woman."[44]

Women were likely to be more directly involved in the management and financial decision making on smaller ranches, whose economies were closely integrated to the common needs of the family. They kept the books for the ranch and the household, recording cattle sales beside the egg money, keeping track of expenses like hay and tea, and documenting births of cattle and babies in their diaries.[45] However, even on some of the larger ranches, such as the Oxley, which at one point in the 1880s held over 100,000 acres of prime lease land, women were involved in management. When the Oxley was reorganized as a private company in 1883 its board of directors comprised Staveley Hill, the Earl of Lathom, George Baird, and all of their wives.[46] It is unknown if any of these women ever saw the ranch first-hand, but on paper, at least, they played a role in its administration. Curiously, influential women have always played a major part on this ranch. From Evelyn Springett, the energetic wife of manager Arthur Springett, in the 1890s, to the fiercely independent owner Elsie Gordon in the 1920s and 1930s, to her granddaughter, Jennifer White, who continues to run the ranch today, women's commitment to the productivity and legacy of this ranch and their direct involvement in its management have enabled the Oxley's survival. Reflecting on women's ongoing role on the Oxley, from its management to the menial tasks required to keep it running, White observed that – as with many other ranches that have been maintained for generations – "this ranch here has been predominantly loved and cared for by women."[47]

As an "economic mechanism," frontier partnerships worked exceedingly well.[48] With the labour of both partners, moderately scaled family ranches proved to be successful and sustainable on the grasslands regions of the West. For some couples trying to establish their lives and livelihoods in a frontier environment, as American historian Cynthia Culver Prescott points out, "the financial necessity of a partner superceded their desire for a romantic companion."[49] When the focus of a relationship was on agricultural production rooted in a system of patriarchy that gave men unlimited authority over women and children, women's status and a family's quality of life were not necessarily improved by the conditions of the frontier. In a study of farm families in North Dakota, Barbara Handy-Marchello notes that "pioneer unions appear to have been primarily economic relationships in which women held (at least nominally) a subordinate position."[50] To a degree this was true on the Canadian ranching frontier; ranch women were not immune to the fundamental inequalities that privileged male ownership of land and assets. Comparatively, however, the frontier period in western Canada occurred much later than it did in various parts of the American West. The notion of companionate marriage, one based on "ideal love" and friendship, was already well established in society at large by the 1890s, when couples began to settle the ranchlands of southern Alberta.[51] Thus many of the couples who came to ranch had intentionally entered into their unions anticipating both the mutual exchange of labour *and* the ideals of companionship and romantic love. When this balance of reciprocity and romance was achieved, women's status within their marriages improved. For many, the ranching frontier of the early twentieth century was an ideal social environment in which the modern marriage thrived. As Elliott West asserts,

> The companionate family and idealized views of children did not develop in response to frontier conditions; they were

> brought westward from elsewhere in Victorian America [and Canada]. . . . [T]he new country did not wear them down or change them dramatically. On the contrary, these attitudes and modes of living flourished because, quite by chance, they were splendidly suited to a setting for which they were never intended – the peculiar world of the frontier West.[52]

The new ideals of companionate marriage combined with the mutual sacrifice and effort that went into establishing homes and ranches on the frontier to enable couples to form the bonds of interdependence, equality, and friendship that led to healthy and productive relationships. Working together strengthened the bonds of marriage. Endless work was the common denominator in many ranchers' relationships, and particularly toward the ends of their lives, partners became reflective and appreciative of each other's contributions. After his wife's death James Fergus, a Montana rancher, credited her with the success of their ranch. He referred to her as the "Madame [who] fails less than I do, works hard, doing nearly all the work for nine men, makes butter, raises chickens, has flowers and plants indoors and out and is always busy."[53] Fergus was a prolific letter writer, and his writing conveys the depth of the partnership that he and his wife eventually shared; clearly his affection for her grew beyond simply respecting her for her hard work. Reflecting on the later years of the couple's life together on their isolated ranch, he wrote: "We were always together and thought far more of each other than we did when we were young. I think people of good sense generally do, having lived so long together they become forgiving and one becomes as it were a necessity to the other, I know it was so with us."[54] Along with the frontier their relationship evolved, from one of economic reciprocity and mutual dependence to one of companionship and deep appreciation.

Partnerships that thrived were based on mutuality and the shared goal of bettering the lives of their families through establishing viable ranching enterprises. The erosion of gendered labour roles facilitated the equality now recognized as beneficial to fulfilling marriages by fostering commonality and an awareness of each person's daily routines and preoccupations. When women were involved in all aspects of ranch life a truer understanding of each other's needs was possible. In her argument that women's riding ability granted them equality, scholar Nancy Young proposes the idea that "to communicate knowledgeably about the tasks, the men, the horses, and the dreams for the future of the ranch, would surely have been of great benefit to a husband and wife."[55] Pioneer rancher Bob Newbolt noted that the mutual affinity for horses he and his wife shared had strengthened their marriage: "Mabel's love for good horses resulted in her persuading me to purchase the beautiful imported Hackney stallion, Romance. This act was to be the means of providing us with plenty of Romance in the years ahead."[56] Mabel and Bob Newbolt integrated their passion for ranching with their commitment to each other: "We both fell in love with our ranch home as well as remaining in love with each other all these years."[57]

Even prior to marriage, women's immediate knowledge of and familiarity with ranch life gave couples a foundation for their relationship. When American cowgirl Agnes Morley Cleaveland was "wooed" by a young cowboy it was the stock that gave them something to talk about while they rode out together: "All of this summer when Tod rode with me we talked of – well, I suppose horses. Maybe we mentioned cows, but it was horses about which most conversations revolved."[58] Since so much of ranch life was spent working, sharing jobs gave couples common interests. The creative fictitious personal ads that the teenage Macleay girls wrote for their *Rocking P Gazette* reflect two realities: that a relationship on a ranch revolved around work and that flexible labour roles were attractive to both men and women.

> Young lady wishes to correspond with Cow-boy who can cook and clean house, lady musical and fond of travel.
>
> Cowpuncher wants wife to run outfit for him. Has good house and a large set of unbreakable dishes.
>
> Handsome cow-boy would like to correspond with a good strong lady who can cook, break horses, chop wood etc.
>
> Wanted before spring; strong young woman, who can haul hay and plow. If good worker will consider marriage.[59]

The desire for a partner with whom to share both work and companionship was a concept familiar to two observant young ranch women who were witness to the romances between the ranch hands and local "school marms."[60]

Although it is daunting to historicize love, the nature of relationships between husbands and wives on the range appears to have been shaped by the intimacy of their working partnership. The working and family lives of ranchers became so interconnected that many sources closely associate love with work. When Richard Copithorne's wife, Sophia, passed away in 1923 at the age of forty-three, adjusting was a struggle for him because he was used to her accompanying him on horseback for ranch work and for sport on organized coyote hunts. His family wrote that "this was a hard blow as she loved to ride over the ranch with him."[61] A lifetime of shared commitment and experience often solidified the deep partnership of a husband and wife. One member of a ranching family from the Twin Butte area remarked on the deep bond that had formed between her parents over a lifetime of ranching together: "When mom died on April 6, 1935 it seemed as though half of Dad died with her. There was no one to give his first strawberry, or his first fish to and he just pined away over the next three years."[62] A poem entitled "You and I" by Catherine Dick, who ranched with her husband near Chain Lakes, Alberta, illustrates the shared experience of a lifetime of ranching with her husband:

We've ridden all the cow-trails on the range,

You and I,

We've rounded up the beef-steers in the fall,

And it's been a busy life,

Filled with joy and work and strife,

But we've weathered it together,

You and I . . .

We've drunk from every crystal sparkling spring,

You and I,

And we have "ridden fence" from dawn to dusk,

We have lunched beneath the blue,

Picked the first spring blooms that grew;
Now the riding days are through, for
 You and I![63]

Another of Dick's poems further emphasizes that mutuality was the fundamental foundation of the family ranch and that the ranch provided an environment in which fulfilling personal relationships thrived:

The hills are all about me now,
 The ranch is much the same,
But my partner drifted off one day –
 It's all in Life's big game.
We had long talks together,
 Our boys, our ranch, our stock;
And now he's gone and I am left,
 Oh, how I miss that talk![64]

As central as the ranch and the need for a working partner was to many relationships, love regularly became an expected component of marriages, particularly after the turn of the century when the previously unbalanced sex ratio began to level off and many family ranches had been established for a decade or more. Rancher Fred Ings wrote from Alberta to his "sweetheart," Edith Scatcherd, whose mother was "very distressed" to see her daughter, and only child, leave London, Ontario, for a new life and marriage in the West:[65]

> You can assure her that I am not marrying you solely for a housekeeper, neither will my little wife be asked to do anything more than the ordinary Canadian girl is accustomed to do in her own home. I think you are too sensible and energetic a girl

> to wish to [wring] your hands all day. I want you to be my best chum to be with me as much as possible.[66]

Their marriage was based on deep friendship and a shared affinity for their home in the heart of ranching country, of which Fred wrote, "This is the country I have lived most of my life in. It is my home. It is mine *it will be ours* . . . free and independent from anyone. If I did not love you as I do I would not ask you to share it with me."[67]

As historian Elliott West concludes, "pioneers poured physical and emotional energy into trying to transplant and nurture traditions in the frontier's fresh soil."[68] Some of these ideals, such the gendered division of labour, were impossible to preserve whereas others, like companionate marriage, took root and flourished. The frontier afforded women opportunities previously thought impossible, and their hard work and resourcefulness, when combined with the support and respect of a true partner, earned them increased status. Though for some the entrenched patriarchal prejudices that limited their ability to control their agricultural assets kept them trapped in abusive marriages, many found ways to gain autonomy. Even when they worked within the context of the family ranch, where men had conventionally held control of primary production and the family's resources, women challenged the limitations socially ascribed to their gender. Many shared decision-making responsibilities with their partners and assumed roles of authority in their households, both in the absence of their husbands or in cooperation with their partners. They took pride in the simple accomplishments associated with maintaining their own homes on their own terms and contributed directly to both the primary and subsistence economies of their families. Hard work was made bearable by the privileges that accompanied the pioneering experience, the freedom from restrictive gender norms, relationships based on shared responsibilities, and the reward of investing oneself in the management of a business that was directly integrated with the labour of each family member and in a marriage that promised love and respect.

CHAPTER FOUR

Childbirth on the Ranching Frontier

In deciding to establish their homes and families on ranches in the largely unsettled West, women knowingly or unknowingly risked their lives as they bore and reared the next generation. Exaggerated frontier fears of the "savage Indian" and roving wild animals were compounded and glorified in contemporary fiction and the popular imagination. However, in reality, giving birth to their children actually posed the greatest mortal threat to western women. Childbirth was a hazard particular to women and arguably the most significant and dangerous life event they faced while living on remote ranches far from a supportive network of friends and family and the security of experienced caregivers or health providers. Through examining ranching women's reproductive experiences, we see the true manifestation of the dangers posed by isolation.

Though pioneer experience could strengthen the bonds of marriage through mutual determination and shared work, pregnancy and labour were trials unique to women. Even when women had a connected, concerned partner, reproductive issues made women aware of the distance between female support networks. Bearing children on the frontier made this typically stalwart class of women physically and emotionally vulnerable. Sources from the period that speak candidly of pregnancy and birth are limited, but those that do discuss these personal and previously taboo subjects illuminate much about the female experience. Consistently, the tone of pioneer ranchers' personal accounts of childbirth is a mix of belief and pride. The tone of disbelief emerges as these women recall the challenges they and their peers had to overcome as they prepared for and gave birth to their children, while a sense of pride imbues their voices as they recall the tenacity, endurance, and grace that they gained as a result of birthing on the frontier.[1] Research on homesteading women's childbirth experiences supports this analysis. Historian Nanci Langford reports similarly dichotomous findings, even going so far as to conclude that childbirth can be viewed as "a microcosm of what homesteading meant for women of this generation" and that accounts of the experience reveal "all that was bad and good about homestead life."[2]

Maternal mortality was one of the greatest dangers for pioneer women. Even as late as 1933, childbirth was second only to tuberculosis as the leading cause of death for women in Canada.[3] When statistics on maternal mortality began to be monitored in Alberta, in the 1920s, the number of deaths was notably higher in rural areas than in urban centres. Multiple factors combined to make childbirth and the postpartum period exceedingly dangerous for rural women: limited personal reproductive knowledge, isolation from supportive women such as relatives or friends, little reprieve from dangerous and strenuous work, the absence of qualified prenatal and maternal care, and the lack of appropriate birthing facilities combined with the significant travel time required to reach them. The conditions of the frontier made bearing and raising children particularly dangerous for ranching women, yet they contributed to women's solidarity in the West.

The challenge of bearing children alone in primitive conditions was exacerbated by many women's ignorance of the birth process and maternal care. Most women on the earliest ranches had no network of experienced female informants. Even as late as the 1920s, the little published material on childbirth and mothering that was available was not applicable to rural women, as it emphasized the "integral" role of medical professionals during delivery and advocated for a scientific approach to child rearing that was impractical in most rural conditions.[4] As a reflection of society at large, the events of the barnyard were separated from those of the bedroom by conventions of modesty. On some ranches propriety dictated that women and girls were not permitted to be present during breeding or calving, even when they were actively involved in other aspects of the operation. This lingering conservative tendency remained intact on some ranches through the generations. Edith Wearmouth, who currently runs the Wineglass Ranch west of Cochrane, Alberta, remarked that when she was growing up in the 1950s "my dad and my grandpa were very strict in that they didn't allow us girls or their wives to be out with the men, so my mom never saw a calf being born until she was well into her sixties."[5] Attempts to protect women's "decency" as late as the 1950s can be interpreted as quaint at best, but restricting women's access to reproductive information during the pioneering years, when they were often left to attend to their own health and that of their children, was fundamentally dangerous.

Lack of readily available reproductive knowledge also resulted from the absence of female companionship and the paucity of forthright conversation about birthing itself. Young families often came west looking for a new beginning, leaving their relatives behind. Women felt this separation from their network of female friends and family most poignantly when pregnant. When Catherine Neil was expecting on a remote southern Alberta sheep ranch, for example, she felt unprepared by her upbringing and by the fact that her extended family were in Scotland:

> As I came from a large city, I had never been on a farm except for a short visit of a week. I was an only girl, and had been raised by one of those reserved Scots mothers, who think it time enough for a girl to learn things about married life, after they are married, always in the hope that she will be at hand to tell all a young wife should know. Unfortunately for me I was married at Medicine Hat, so my mother was far away.[6]

Letter writing kept women connected to their family and friends in the East. However, as Langford's research suggests, women's writing seldom revealed any information about pregnancy, though out of necessity it might mention the event of the birth itself.[7] Correspondence regarding the 1907 birth of Claudia Gardiner on the Wineglass Ranch brusquely related that "Alice [the mother] is alright but it was an awfully long time but came naturally in the end. Got to fix up the house, get lunch and pack so no time for more."[8] Even women familiar with livestock and the biological processes of animals were generally reticent to share information about reproductive issues.[9] When writing to a friend concerning a neighbour's birth experience, Monica Hopkins – who typically gave a blunt depiction

4.1 A baby in diapers takes the reins on the Key Horse Ranch (c.1906). Reproduced with permission of Glenbow Archives.

of events – was elusive: "She knew what had happened, or at any rate what was going to happen, if it hadn't already happened. (I hope you can follow my happenings.)"[10] Limited opportunities to connect with other women and the lack of readily available and forthright practical information for birthing and caring for their children compounded the challenges of starting a family on the ranching frontier.

Rancher Doris Burton's experience was representative of those who struggled physically and emotionally to bear their children on remote ranches because they had been ill-prepared by their families and society. Written in reflection, both the introduction and conclusion of Burton's memoir explicitly emphasize her lack of reproductive knowledge and her personal opinion that raising girls innocent of the "facts of life" was detrimental to women's health and autonomy. Born in 1910 and raised in a seemingly egalitarian ranching and outfitting family near Waterton, Alberta, Burton grew up continually surrounded by both domestic and wild animals. Yet, as a girl she never witnessed a live birth, nor did she ever ask her parents where the new animals came from. Though from a young age she was entrusted with empowering responsibilities such as tending camp and wrangling pack horses alone for days in the wilderness, Burton was emotionally and physically unprepared for her marriage, at age sixteen, and for the babies that followed shortly thereafter. When her son was born, on October 21, 1927, following "a very complicated delivery," she "had never seen a baby changed or nursed."[11] In the conclusion of her memoirs, she stridently argued that girls deserve to grow up and become informed before they reproduce. Drawing from a multitude of rich life experiences that had thrust her into traditionally masculine domains, such as cougar hunting with hounds, breaking her own horses, and running a ranch, Burton emphasized that informed motherhood above all else was the most important element of women's emancipation. Because both of her children were born when she was very young and living in primitive conditions, in a shack on a grazing lease in the mountains, she suffered permanent physical damage because she lacked the nutrition and the respite from work needed to bear and raise them sufficiently. Burton advised that "if a child is involved, it has the right from conception on to a mother during its unborn nine months, where her body is ready to supply the building of the child and not deplete her health."[12] She advocated physical, mental, and spiritual maturity and preparedness for taking on the task of mothering – wise advice from a woman who raised her own children under challenging conditions, yet highly idealistic for the circumstances of her generation of ranching women.

Even women in the most advantaged positions within the ranching order faced frontier conditions that were not particular to status. To a degree, women were equalized by their birthing experiences. As Elliot West notes in his analysis of parenting in the American West, all women "were expected to see to the thousands of details of child care while tackling the demanding jobs of frontier homemaking. Even the luckiest felt the strain."[13] Unlike Burton, Evelyn Springett had domestic help and the means to live comfortably on the ranch her husband managed, but even so, she recalled being overwhelmed and unprepared for caring for her infant daughter:

4.2 Frank and Josephene Bedingfeld pose with baby Josephene for a family photo (1914). Reproduced with permission of Glenbow Archives.

> A puny little mite she cried incessantly for the first few months of her life. I seemed to have plenty of nourishment for my baby, but she did not thrive; probably because I did not handle her aright. I had been ill off and on for months and was pitifully thin and run-down; and I had no one to advise me, either before or after her advent.[14]

Without appropriate prenatal and postpartum care, and without either the support of family or the security of being well informed, women in the simplest range shacks and on the most prominent open-range ranches simply did the best they could to meet the needs of their children.

The amount of physical work women performed during their pregnancies and during the postpartum recovery period changed little from the extent of their typical duties on the ranch. Out of necessity, pregnant women and new mothers remained active and engaged in the process of sustaining their families, homes, and ranches. Often this entailed physically demanding domestic work: hauling water, tending fires, and preparing meals were inevitably part of their daily routine. Most women also continued a degree of involvement in the functions of the ranch at large. Both housework and ranch work posed a hazard to pregnant women, but a break from their responsibilities was not an option when there was no extended family or hired help to provide assistance to their husbands. Women's contributions to their family economies were not curtailed by pregnancy. Accustomed to participating in ranch work alongside their husbands, most women chose to continue to ride and work, particularly when the alternative was to remain alone in an isolated ranch house. Violet LaGrandeur, who ranched with her husband in southern Alberta, recalled that she had ridden right up to the end of her first pregnancy, in May 1912:

> It was time to trail a load of horses to Medicine Hat. Emery said he would be away for four days with the [h]orses. I said, "Okay, so will Violet LaGrandeur." I wasn't going to stay alone out there. We saddled our horses, struck out with the string of horses that were to be shipped. I am sure that these broncs never walked a mile the whole fifty miles. After we got to the stockyards at Medicine Hat, we rode to the Royal Hotel which was run by John Quail. I dismounted, the first time out of the saddle since daylight that morning. I was pretty weary as I was expecting our first born in about two months.[15]

For many women who remained active during their pregnancies, being stuck in the house with a newborn baby was harder to endure than the injuries sustained from ranch work. Rancher Doris Fenton, who kept up her workload on the ranch even after her children were born, was not fazed by being bucked off a colt she was training – something that had occurred because Fenton "didn't have strength back in . . . [her] legs yet because Barb [her daughter] was only a month old."[16] Fenton later recalled that after the birth of her son, Carl, what bothered her more than being thrown from a horse was that "Stuart was hauling straw and I couldn't go. I was watching out the window in the kitchen, bawling because I couldn't be with him."[17]

Like LaGrandeur, Fenton, and others, Catherine Neil was engaged in a working partnership with her husband, and pregnancy did not limit her involvement in ranch operations. As a young woman helping to run a sheep ranch in remote southeastern Alberta in the early 1900s, Neil had multiple accidents during her pregnancies. She participated in all elements of ranch work, but one of her injuries occurred while she was simply preparing supper and fell down the steep stairs leading to the cellar. Typically, however, it was handling livestock that posed the greatest physical threat to women. Toward the end of the same pregnancy, Neil was assisting her husband as he worked the sheep through a corral. She was standing outside of the enclosure trying to keep the sheep from jumping the fence when one of the panels fell on her. The sheep then escaped, trampling her in the process.[18] Neil's most serious injury was sustained during her third pregnancy. While she was putting the horses in the stable for the night, one broke away and tried to get out the door past her. It head-butted her in the abdomen, sent her flying, and then stepped on her and broke her arm. With two small children at home, Neil was desperate for assistance. A year earlier, she had taken in three girls from a neighbouring family while their mother recovered from an infection obtained during childbirth. In return, the family sent their fourteen-year-old daughter over to help. This was "a blessing," according to Neil.[19] When she later had to undergo abdominal surgery to repair internal injuries caused by the accident, the girl again stayed to care for the children while Neil healed.[20] It was this mutual exchange of labour and goodwill that enabled women to make it through the daunting ordeal of childbirth and childrearing while responsible for so many other duties as well.

While there were hazards associated with the physical nature of the work required by ranch women, this work also kept them physically and mentally prepared to meet other challenges. Although, as mentioned above, standards of appropriateness differed from ranch to ranch, some women were likely to witness and aid in the birth of their livestock. In an age where little reproductive information was disseminated to women and when they were separated from other females who could share their own personal knowledge of the facts of life, it was involvement with livestock that provided women with invaluable and critical life lessons. Catherine Neil was responsible for assisting the sheep during complicated births because her hands were better suited than the men's to working in the birth canal. This active involvement led to several of her accidents, but the experience also provided her with essential reproductive knowledge. And she clearly valued this education. Later, she commented that "it was during this first lambing season that I got my first lesson in midwifery."[21] She was further educated in midwifery when her first child came earlier than expected and the birth was attended by a Mrs. Slawson, who acted as the neighbourhood midwife.[22]

Typically, when possible, ranch women made arrangements to travel to the nearest hospital or birthing facility shortly before their expected date of delivery or had a doctor or midwife notified once labour began and brought to the ranch for the delivery. However, with the great distance between towns, the expansive size of many outfits, and the unpredictable nature of birth itself, it was all too common for a woman to labour at home without assistance for all or part of the birth. In 1907, Augusta Hoffman and her siblings were the only attendants for the birth of their sister. Hoffman recalled that "in all her pain" her mother "asked us children to pray for her as that was all we could do."[23] Other women were not as lucky, and their tragedies affected the decision making of those around them. In the Porcupine Hills in the 1890s, isolation and impassable conditions trapping them in their remote ranch home during a spring flood led to the death of both a labouring woman and her baby.[24] The woman's neighbour, Evelyn Springett of the New Oxley Ranch, was cautioned by the event and made arrangements to go to Fort Macleod for the birth of her own first child. Yet, despite her advanced planning, she laboured primarily alone when the baby came five weeks earlier than expected:

> At about 5 o'clock in the morning I could bear it no longer, and one of the cowboys went galloping off to the station sixteen miles away, to fetch the station agent's wife, a good soul who had some experience in a slum district in England. . . . Though she was vastly better than no one at all, I shall never forget those awful hours before the doctor arrived. The heat was terrible and I was covered by flies.[25]

After this harrowing experience, Springett's family encouraged her to spend her second "confinement" in the comfort of her well-to-do brother's home in Winnipeg rather than risk labour on the ranch a second time.[26]

Those who travelled away from their ranches to birth were occasionally more comfortable and provided with better care than they may have received at home. However, often the journey itself was hazardous to the well-being of mother and child. Weather, distance, and trail conditions were the biggest factors that determined the comfort of a labouring woman's trip to the doctor. Monica Hopkins wrote of the experience of her neighbour, Mrs. Bolt, who had "had her babe under the most unpleasant circumstances, though they seem fairly ordinary out here."[27] The labouring woman was being transported by buckboard to the doctor when it became evident that the baby would arrive before the trip could be completed. The travellers made it to a neighbour's house "on the gallop," getting there just in time for the baby to be delivered – while the baby's father "was having hysterics in the stable."[28] Hopkins wrote: "Freda said the buckboard never missed a stump or a stone on the road. She was bumping around so much she hardly noticed the pain, she was so afraid she would be thrown out."[29] As Catherine Neil recalled, unforeseen emergencies could also disrupt plans to have a baby in town. Expecting her second child, Neil and her husband were en route from their ranch to catch the train to Lethbridge when they spotted a prairie fire and had to turn back to fight it. After the fire was out they continued on, arriving just in time for the baby to be born the following morning.[30] Other women were less fortunate. For many women, travel proved more than they were physically able to withstand. While travelling from Calgary to Kamloops, where her husband was to manage the Senator Bostock Ranch, Elizabeth Callaway gave birth to her sixth child in a railway station. Shortly after their arrival in Kamloops, Callaway passed away.[31]

Women's tales of discomfort and close calls during home births served as cautionary advice for their contemporaries, prompting some – but only those who had the opportunity provided by location and means – to labour in hospital. Although she never did have any children, Hopkins wrote that "I have heard so many appalling stories of abnormal births since I came out here that I have made up my mind to spend the nine months in a hospital to be on the safe side."[32] However, turn-of-the-century medical standards and practitioners could be inadequate, unprofessional, or unsanitary. Maternal morbidity was not necessarily decreased by the presence of a doctor, and hospital staff often interfered with a mother's ability to care for her child as she wished.[33] Common risks associated with pioneer women's births, such as infection and toxemia, can be attributed in part to suspect frontier hospital conditions. May Dodds Ings, the first wife of rancher Fred Ings, succumbed to an infection commonly dubbed "childbed fever," shortly after giving birth to their son in a hospital in High River in 1898. Two other women at this hospital died in similar circumstances at the same time.[34] Tragically, the risk of maternal death was so great that Ings, like many other women, had prepared her affairs prior to delivery just in case she did not survive. When her husband, who had been away on a horse-selling trip at the time of the birth, returned to the ranch some months after her death he found a letter laden with pathos, saying goodbye and explicitly detailing how she wanted her child to be raised:

> I am writing this to you today, not because I am feeling ill but because it relieves my mind to know that if anything does happen I shall have said the few things I wished. Darling if the little one comes and lives and I should not, I know that for its mother's sake you will do the best you can for it. But because a child needs a woman's care I should like sister May to have it to bring up till it was old enough to be a companion to you. She would be the only one who I could trust *our* little one to. Then whatever you do with my things only keep my watch for my child – it will be old enough to be valuable then. Dearest love you have been so good to me and I know you love me truly, but some day you may meet some good woman who will be happy to make you comfortable. Then dear remember I should wish you to marry again, for I should have had your love first and I should not be jealous when it['s] for your good. Oh love good-bye. I don't know what makes me feel that it is to be a good-bye, but something seems to tell me to write this to you. You are so good dear far better than I and I know that if God takes me to him you will come to me there bye and bye. Live so you will my darling and bring up the little one to be proud and tell it of me and give it the best education you can. Kiss me darling; I love you so much. So much. Your Wife.[35]

4.3 Edith Ings, pregnant with her second daughter, feeding an orphaned foal on the lawn outside her home (c.1912). Reproduced with permission of Glenbow Archives.

Seemingly as an afterthought, she had scrawled across the bottom of the page, "Dear either bury me at home or out here near *you*."[36] On the frontier, women knew that anything was possible; unfortunately, childbirth often manifested their worst fears.

In most cases a lack of funds, the inability to leave one's responsibilities at home, or the absence of a facility nearby prompted women to birth at home. However, for many the sense of autonomy and security they felt at home was simply preferable to being confined in hospital. When she was expecting her second child, Edith Ings travelled the twelve miles to town and returned home after the doctor advised her that the birth was imminent, preferring to labour in the familiar and comfortable surroundings of her summer ranch house in the hills rather than in the hospital. The child born that day, Constance Ings Loree, recounted that "when she was expecting me to be born, she drove down in the buggy to see the doctor, knowing her time was close. He advised her to either stay down, or return to the ranch immediately, which she did. I was born at Sunset [Ranch] that same day, before the doctor arrived."[37] For all the tragedy and challenges associated with bearing children on the frontier, most women, remarkably, whether assisted by medical professionals or not, lived to raise their children on the range.

Pioneer ranch women were tested by birthing and tending to their children. However, it was in overcoming frontier conditions that they developed the tenacity to establish their homes, families, friendships, and communities in the West. They strategized to deal with their isolation, turning to one another where and when they could for birthing support or postpartum care. But in the earliest phases of settlement in ranching districts there were simply too few women and they were too recently arrived to have developed networks of mutual aid. Writing of more established agricultural communities in the American Midwest in the early twentieth century, historian Mary Neth notes that "life transitions such as births or deaths, often required economic assistance as well as emotional support. Neighbourhood and kin networks provided this support."[38] However, in the earliest phases of pioneer ranching, in the 1880s and 1890s, these networks were seldom available; the provision of adequate support for new mothers often took money of their own. For all of the levelling effects of the frontier, this is one area where having money directly contributed to an increased quality of life. Hired domestic help was invaluable in making

4.4 Hired help was welcome, especially for mothers who were actively involved with ranch work, as was Josephene Bedingfeld (1912). Reproduced with permission of Glenbow Archives.

the postpartum period more manageable and was virtually ubiquitous among the most privileged ranch women, such as Luella Goddard of the Bow River Horse Ranche. Hired girls, nurses, and governesses – or "Lady Helps," as they were called by the Lynch-Staunton household – were common on ranches that could afford them.[39] However, securing long-term help was a problem that plagued frontier households. Staff turnover rates were high, as many young women who came west as employees soon married and established families and ranches of their own. As an alternative to hired help – or as a supplement to it – sisters, mothers, or friends made extended visits from distant homes to provide companionship and ease the burden of mothering on the frontier. Elizabeth Lane, who had married Bar U Ranch manager George Lane in 1885, recalled gratefully that when her eight children were young, her sister Alvira had spent "a good deal of time with me" on the Lanes' recently acquired and remote ranch on Willow Creek.

The isolated and self-sufficient nature of their lives led most women to believe that they were expected to bear their children stoically and independently. However, where possible, women expressed great solidarity by assisting one another with their births, and it was in this mutual assistance that women formed the bonds that began to build communities. In 1887, Lily Young, who had recently settled in the Springbank district west of Calgary, was forced to deliver her own baby while her husband attempted to get a doctor. Fortunately, she had prepared herself in anticipation of an unassisted birth by soliciting the advice and instruction of her doctor prior to leaving Ontario. Although she managed the birth by herself, she was adamant that no woman should have to give birth alone, and she became a birth assistant to over one hundred babies in the community.[40] Like other community-oriented midwives, Young not only provided help during the delivery itself, but also often assisted a family in getting ready for a new arrival by helping with housework or food preparation – invaluable aid to a new mother, particularly under the demands of frontier conditions where providing meals was an all-consuming task in itself. Another laywoman, Bertha McCarthy, locally dubbed "the only doctor the Twin Butte area ever had," presided over many births.[41] Like other women in her unofficial position of responsibility, McCarthy felt obligated to help her sisters in need despite the associated risks. In 1911 she brought her own baby with her on a wintery night to aid with a delivery and her daughter's minor cold turned to pneumonia and she died shortly thereafter.[42] Because women on isolated ranches and homesteads were dependent on the goodwill of their neighbours for assistance, those with the will and competence to aid their fellow women were highly respected members of their communities. While they received little remuneration for their services, they were often repaid in food, livestock, or the simple admiration and deep appreciation of their peers. A Saskatchewan rancher, Pansy White-Brekhus, recalled the home birth of her younger brother: "The old lady that lived next to us couldn't talk English – she spoke Norwegian, and she came down. She was a midwife and she was pretty capable. And after, whenever she saw my brother, she would say, 'That's my boy.'"[43] The bonds created by a sense of shared responsibility for the well-being of mothers and children transcended barriers of language and ethnicity and facilitated community building on the ranching frontier.

Children created a common bond among women. Differences in social standing, country of origin, and language were diminished by the presence of a baby and the recognition of the shared experience of the challenges that accompanied mothering on an isolated frontier. After a particularly lonely period, Catherine Neil recalled, she felt relief and euphoria upon meeting her first "Canadian" baby and his mother:

> I visited another of the early settlers, a Mrs. Clark. She was a young woman with a tiny baby, and I managed to tell her all my trials. When we met we ran to each other, and put our arms around each other's neck, and just had a good cry. All the hunger and longing we each had to speak to another woman, and had stifled for so long, gave way, and we felt better after our cry. She led me to a little cot fashioned out of an orange box, and daintily hung with muslin, and there I saw the first little Canadian baby.[44]

Ranch women's vulnerability was illuminated by the conditions and risks associated with childbirth. However, it was also this circumstance that encouraged them to seek out solidarity with other women and strive to improve health care for themselves and their families. Despite the challenges and threats to their own personal safety, most women reinforced the significance of their contributions to their households while they were pregnant. A major theme of this book is that, as previous chapters have demonstrated, women were producers as well as reproducers, but their reproductive labour in the form of bearing and providing for the next generation of ranchers was an especially poignant part of the pioneer experience.[45] Indeed, providing a future full of opportunities for their children was the motivation behind many women's decision to ranch in the West. The first generation of ranch women garnered great respect from their contemporaries because of their dedication to mothering. Old-time cowboy T. B. Long eulogistically praised the efforts of frontier mothers, commenting that "those pioneer women were hardy, game and tough. I sometimes think they could stand more hardship than a man. . . . [Y]es these pioneer women accomplished miracles and yet they thought of it only in terms of their duty as homemakers."[46] Yet perhaps pioneer mothering represented desire more than duty. Women came to the West desiring opportunity for themselves and their families and sought solutions to overcome the hardships involved in making this desire a reality.

CHAPTER FIVE

Clothing and Saddles: Manifestations of Adaptation

One concrete way to explore how women adapted to life in the West is to examine material artefacts such as clothing and saddles. History has captured the image of the newly arrived English rancher in his tailored suit and necktie topped by a Stetson hat, or wearing his bowler hat with woolly chaps. Less known is how women combined their former ideals of dress with the new realities of ranch life. By examining how women dressed we can see how they employed similar adaptive strategies as their male counterparts while they assimilated cultural components and environmental elements of the Alberta ranching frontier.

The image from Wild West shows of a "cowgirl" in full, flamboyant western regalia has been popularized more as a way to titillate and entertain than to reflect how women actually dressed. As much as possible the first generation of ranching women attempted to maintain the manners of the Old World through their choice of traditional dress, but out of necessity they made concessions to practicality by gearing themselves appropriately for the range. On most ranches, conservative decorum dictated to some degree what women wore. Late-Victorian and early-Edwardian tradition mandated that women, particularly those from the middle and upper classes, wore a full wardrobe. This costume typically included a corset, bodice, and assortment of petticoats, topped by an ankle-length dress. Often an apron was worn as a protective addition to the ensemble. While this attire was functional for housework and limited barnyard chores, it restricted the work that women could perform with safety and efficiency on the ranch at large. Riding apparel was originally composed of a tailored, tight-fitting jacket, modelled after the corseted bodices of classical Victorian fashion, and a long, very full skirt suitable for keeping a woman modestly covered while riding side-saddle. Even this ensemble, designed for horseback riding, posed limitations on the extent of women's activities. The transition to clothes more appropriate to an active ranching lifestyle, replete with rough riding and working with livestock, was gradual. There was no mass revolution in "ranch fashion"; rather, each individual modified her wardrobe as necessary to suit her social position, tastes, and activity level. This fluidity of style makes photographs of ranch women from this period notoriously hard to date, as women's style of dress differed from person to person and according to occasion. There was no definitive point when fashions changed. Some women were strictly practical in their choice of attire, as were an American mother and daughter duo who independently ran an enterprising ranching operation south of Moose Jaw. A travelling reporter in 1902 found these "refined, good looking" ladies "dressed in good fitting men's clothing, and they excused themselves by saying they were doing men's work and couldn't do it while wearing women's clothing."[1] Others preferred to remain more traditionally attired and found ways to modify their feminine wardrobes to suit both function and formality. On most southern Alberta ranches the predominant style of dress was a hybrid of late-Victorian fashion and characteristic western function. Edith Ings, born to a high-society Ontario family, combined Eastern styles such as English riding breeches and boots and her much-loved hound's tooth riding jacket with typical cowboy accoutrements such as a wide-brimmed hat, silk scarf, and gauntlet gloves that sported fringe and Indigenous beadwork.[2]

Ranch women who maintained the standards of femininity that they deemed fitting to their station in life attempted to stay up to date with current Eastern fashion even while dressing for work. When occasion permitted, they enjoyed dressing in their finest. Newspaper accounts of early balls and dances recognized the glamour and air of decorum that women strove to bring to the frontier by maintaining formal customs, manners, and fashion, and photographs indicate that they attempted to do this in their everyday dress as well.[3] Thus the same woman who rode astride

5.1 Miss E. M. Shackerly in formal winter riding attire (c.1916). Reproduced with permission of Glenbow Archives.

sporting cowboy boots and rowelled spurs could be seen corseted, in a fitted, high-collared dress, and topped with furs when making a social call. This unpredictable, or timeless, nature of ranch women's fashion makes photographs from this period notoriously hard to date. Women's style of dress differed from person to person and according to occasion, blending modern trends with tradition and functional gear with high fashion.

Even those not required to perform "men's work" found it necessary to adopt clothes more suited to their new lifestyle and environment. Evelyn Springett, who wore the traditional riding habit fitting her position as a privileged ranch manager's wife in the 1890s, abandoned convention in favour of practicality after a particular incident revealed how unsuitable, and indeed unsafe, her attire was for life on the remote foothills range west of Fort Macleod. One of Springett's weekly tasks was to ride or drive nine miles to fetch the mail. She rode in a side saddle in "the long, clinging, old-fashioned riding habit."[4] On one particularly hot prairie day her horse stumbled and both horse and rider fell. Although they were unhurt, her horse refused to be caught and she attempted to walk back to the ranch, fearing for her safety due to the threat of wild and dangerously unpredictable range cattle. She soon discovered the impractical nature of her

5.2 A practical ensemble (c.1890–1905). Reproduced with permission of Glenbow Archives.

ensemble, for she could barely manage the terrain in her restrictive dress and when she finally managed to catch her horse she had to walk another mile until she found a boulder large enough to assist her to mount. In her memoirs, Springett recalls this event as a specific turning point in her choice of dress: "I must say that shortly after this I took to using a stock saddle and thereafter felt much safer and independent."[5] And presumably, she adopted a split skirt to accommodate her new riding style.

Even if they still rode side-saddle in a full habit and skirt on occasion, by the early 1900s many ranch women had adapted their wardrobes to include split skirts. As early as the 1890s, saddle makers and popular catalogue companies, such as Eaton's, offered women's western riding outfits, made up of wide-legged divided skirts suited to riding astride. Wearing clothing that facilitated riding with one leg on either side of the horse made practical sense for several reasons. Being able to ride more athletic, high-spirited ranch horses enabled women to participate in a wider range of activities, such as sorting cattle and riding for sport, and gave them the confidence of knowing they could travel long distances on isolated terrain more securely. Springett was not the only western woman to learn from experience that it was imperative to replace the conventional riding habit and side saddle with split skirts and a stock saddle. Maude Kemmis, who ranched in the Pincher Creek district in the 1890s, always rode side-saddle but realized from experience the hazards of skirts. One day her usually reliable horse Captain "stumbled badly, throwing her to the off side where she hung, upside down. Her new riding habit skirt caught on the pommel of the saddle. Maude put her hands over her head to protect it and Captain trotted on. Finally just as the waist band gave way, J. K. [her husband, who was riding ahead of her] looked back saying 'What on earth are you doing there?' 'Picking daisies of course, catch my horse!'"[6] Edith Ings, a Nanton-area rancher, also learned the shortcomings of her full-skirted riding habit after falling off her horse. On one of her four-mile return trips from town, the cinch holding the side saddle on her horse broke. Ings was obliged to make the rest of the trip precariously balanced sideways on her horse's bare back, as her skirt prevented her from riding astride.[7] In Montana, Evelyn Cameron found that most ranch horses were terrified by the approach of a woman in billowing skirts and that, even when assisted in mounting, to swing one's leg up across the pommel at the front of the saddle often prompted these horses to buck. She wrote that "it was clear that to be perfectly independent I must ride old 'dead heads' which were not at all to my taste. I therefore determined to ride astride."[8]

The divided skirt, while fundamentally changing the way a woman rode, was not a drastic departure from the traditional habit. Women continued to be plagued by the problem of spooking their horses with their billowing clothing or by having their skirts dangerously tangled in their tack. Even updated riding outfits designed for riding astride were not always appropriate for the rugged conditions of the frontier. Among their shortcomings was the fact that they required more maintenance to keep clean than basic work clothes. Monica Hopkins, who learned to ride shortly after arriving at her Priddis ranch home in 1909, wrote, "I have an awfully nice habit, really far too good to wear all the time. I shall have to get a cheap riding skirt which the 'mail order' catalogues have listed."[9] She soon became a competent horsewoman, accustomed to wearing clothes suitable for the environment, but on special occasion was thrilled to have "the very latest in riding habits."[10] On a social call to a new English bride

5.3 Riding astride in a stock saddle, Mrs. Ed Hartt looks at home on the range (c.1904–16). Reproduced with permission of Glenbow Archives.

in the area, Hopkins discovered the near impossibility of keeping clothes pristine when horses were the primary means of transportation: "I had warned Billie that I wanted to be taken by the very driest of trails, no splashing through creeks or wallowing in muskegs for me. I was willing to scale hilltops but go where there was water I would not. My habit is 'washable' but I had no desire to wash and iron it for months to come and as Billie is back again on the wash tub he was almost equally anxious to keep it from getting soiled."[11] As luck would have it, she came off her horse in a muddy bog and the anticipated visit was called off in favour of returning home to soak her "beautiful habit" in the wash basin. Accordingly, "the ride home was not as sedate as the going and I gaily splashed through mud holes without a thought to the mud that was getting on me; a little more wouldn't hurt anyway."[12] The reality of range conditions, such as unpredictable terrain, and the circumstances of frontier households, including laborious washing methods, increasingly made it all the more appealing to wear practical clothing.

In some circumstances, there was resistance to the revolution in women's clothing. Evelyn Cameron, a remarkably progressive rancher and photographer, recalled that when she made her first public appearance in a split-skirt "California riding costume," in the late 1890s, she was threatened with arrest in Miles City, Montana, and "after riding into town forty-eight miles from the ranch, I was much amused at the laughing and giggling girls who stood staring at my costume as I walked about."[13] Mrs. Charles Gage, who worked alongside her husband to establish their ranch in the Stavely, Alberta, area in 1903, preferred practical dress, but was aware of the traditional social mores her husband favoured. Her daughter recounts:

> Mother took her place with Dad in the fields, handling at first four head of oxen and later horses. That was before the day of slacks for women. Mother soon found trousers the most suitable garb for field work, but always tied to the hames of the harness was a skirt for a quick change in case anyone came along. The era was still Victorian, and Dad would have been mortified if a stranger had seen Mother wearing overalls.[14]

Even when cognizant of resistance to their masculine apparel, women were motivated by comfort, practicality, and personal circumstance when they chose their mode of dress.

Ranch women all throughout the West chose to adopt practical clothing when it facilitated their expanded roles on the range. American cowgirl Agnes Morley Cleaveland described her drastic departure from traditional clothing in the mid-1890s, emphasizing that her rejection of the side saddle and the restrictive feminine wardrobe that accompanied it was a major step toward her "emancipation":

> First, I discarded, or rather refused to adopt, the sunbonnet, conventional headgear of my female neighbors. When I went unashamedly about under a five-gallon (not ten-gallon) Stetson, many an eyebrow was raised; then followed a double-breasted blue flannel shirt, with white pearl buttons, frankly unfeminine.

> In time came blue denim knockers worn *under* a short blue denim skirt. Slow evolution (or was it decadence?) toward a costume suited for immediate needs. Decadence having set in, the descent from the existing standards of female modesty to purely human comfort and convenience was swift.[15]

In response to Cleaveland's unconventional apparel, her brother offered the weak threat of not riding with her – a threat that, out of necessity, he was promptly forced to retract. Often what was deemed acceptable in one community was seen as radical in another. As Teresa Jordan points out in her study of American ranch women, most had limited knowledge of women in other areas. This was also true of women in isolated Canadian ranching communities; thus, each woman assumed her own modifications to suit her particular needs and situation.[16]

While some people were uncomfortable with women's departure from traditional dress, most were realistic about the safety and efficiency provided by women ranchers riding astride like their male counterparts. According to an Ings family story, as told to me my by mother, Edith Ings was encouraged to ride a stock saddle by her husband, Fred, who was concerned for her safety. Although Edith was an accomplished horsewoman who had ridden to the hounds in a side saddle in Ontario, Fred suggested she adopt a more secure seat by riding astride when she began jumping barbwire fences in her side saddle in Alberta. Of course, as a tragic incident from the Longview area illustrates, jumping wire fences remained dangerous no matter what style of riding was involved. Rancher Arthur Dick was killed in plain view of his wife and six children when he lost control of a colt he was riding and it jumped a wire gate. He was thrown to the ground and never regained consciousness.[17] On the range one could merely lower the risks, not eliminate them completely. However, despite the inherent danger of horseback riding, the gradual evolution in riding apparel helped to further women's independence by making their essentially egalitarian means of transportation – the horse – safer, more enjoyable, and more accessible.

A woman's saddle and her style of riding were just as indicative of her level of assimilation to the ranching frontier as was her style of dress. Many women had been educated and experienced equestrians prior to their arrival in the West; however, they had been trained to ride side-saddle, a

5.4 This rider looks ready to go to work on a big, solid stock horse (no date). Reproduced with permission of Glenbow Archives.

style thought to be suitable for modest women. The art of riding side-saddle was thought to embody grace and elegance, yet in reality it was (and is) a challenging and athletic practice. Women on side saddles could keep up with their male counterparts, who rode astride: they jumped, galloped, rode across rough country, and hunted with hounds. Initially, even on the ranching frontier, side-saddle was the standard mode of riding for women. Photographs illustrate the juxtaposition of women posed elegantly on their English side saddles against a backdrop of western rangeland. Even though stock saddles were requisite for cowboys and male ranchers, women rode side-saddle as a reflection of their cultural origins. It was a distinctive part of their Anglo heritage and a reflection of femininity. Owning a saddle was a source of pride and a reflection of maturity. When Bella Chappelle was eleven years old, in the 1890s, she stayed with a family friend near her ranch on Heath Creek, Alberta. The friend gifted her a side saddle that she no longer used. Chappelle recalled, "I was so proud I could hardly sleep."[18] Even when they performed strenuous ranch work, some women enjoyed the tradition of riding side-saddle and never adapted to a stock saddle. Abigail Sexsmith, who independently raised horses and cattle on her family's original homestead near High River, continued to ride side-saddle her entire life. Sexsmith even rode for miles "with skill and grace" on her niece Elsie Gordon's ranch when she was eighty-six years old.[19] Mrs. Gordon, too, rode side-saddle throughout her entire ranching career.[20] In the Parkland district in the early 1900s, a teacher, Miss Claire, rode side-saddle – "a style that seemed very genteel and strange to most of the students, although the Broomfield girls at first rode that way, and so did Mrs. Til Fisher who could take her part in the round-up with the men."[21]

As more women began to ride the ranges of southern Alberta at the turn of the twentieth century, several types of saddles were designed specifically to meet their needs. Some women still preferred to ride side-saddle but needed and wanted to ride many long, hard miles on their ranches. A sturdier, western-style side saddle was developed to provide for this market. Western side-saddles were made with heavier skirting than their English-style counterparts in order to be more durable and resilient to hard riding conditions, and they sported intricate tooling on the leather much like the decorative work on a stock saddle. Some used double rigging, with a front and back cinch, which helped the saddle stay in place when women rode rank horses or covered rough terrain. These saddles sometimes incorporated a pocket or pouch designed to carry small items in the saddle skirt or had saddle strings with which to tie on a load needed for long days in the saddle.[22] This cross-bred saddle is a remarkable symbol

5.5 Note the double rigging on the sturdy western side saddle and the western headstall (c.1890–1905). Reproduced with permission of Glenbow Archives.

of the marriage of eastern tradition with western function. Indeed, it reflects the role of ranch women as cultural mediators; through their appearance, women maintained a sense of tradition and femininity while they engaged in the same pursuits as the men – chasing cows, exploring new ground, and becoming at home in the West.

Although almost ubiquitous among ranch women of Anglo origin during the 1880s and 1890s, the side saddle was beginning to disappear by the turn of the century. Evelyn Cameron, who had been one of the first to ride in a split skirt in Montana, gave compelling reasons for women to give up the side saddle: for one, "sidesaddles are of little use in the west except on 'plumb gentle' horses."[23] In 1914, describing what she felt to be the authentic "cowgirl," Cameron wrote, "For some twenty years past there have been cowgirls on Western ranches who are the feminine counterparts of the cowboys – riding in similar saddles, on similar horses, for the purpose of similar duties, which they do, in fact, efficiently perform. The abolition

5.6 Miss Lucille Mulhall, champion lady steer roper. This Western stock saddle is strong enough for roping (1912). Reproduced with permission of Glenbow Archives.

of the side saddle was naturally the first step towards the creation of the cowgirl."[24] When women were required, or chose, to participate in rigorous and dangerous ranch work, such as roping calves for branding or breaking young horses, they were most effective when dressed and mounted appropriately. A stock saddle that used heavy single or double rigging and had a thick horn attached to a sturdy tree was most suitable for roping and holding cattle and riding rough-stock. However essential for ranch work, this type of saddle was cumbersome and required a certain degree of strength to wield. As rancher Doris Burton recalls in her memoirs: "I only saw one cowgirl who could hold a skittish bronc and swing her heavily loaded saddle on with a one hand grip on the horn, while the cinches almost caved the shuddering bronc in on the other side. I would have liked to have strength like that, but not the vocabulary that went with it."[25] As women began to phase out of side saddles, demand grew for a western saddle designed specifically for women.

This next evolution produced a practical lightweight saddle that could be found in use from Texas to Alberta.[26] This saddle was comfortable and close-fitting, much like an English saddle, but was stouter and had a high cantle that made it more secure. It had less rigging (cinches and plates to fasten it) than a man's saddle, contributing to its light weight and enabling women to conveniently tack up their horses themselves. The trademark characteristic of these saddles was the brass or nickel horn, an attractive feature that unfortunately reduced the structural strength of the saddle tree, making these pretty saddles unsuitable for roping heavy cattle or horses.[27] My own family had one of these brass-horned saddles, gifted to my granny on her eighth birthday from her mother and passed on to my mother, who rode in it until her death in 2014.

Another interesting innovation in stock saddles was the "mother and child saddle." This saddle was designed to accommodate a mother riding with a small child seated in front of her, a common and essential practice in ranching country, particularly prior to the advent of motorized vehicles. An example of this style could be found at our Trail's End Ranch west of Nanton, Alberta.[28] It was still in use up until the late 1980s. This saddle sported a long seat, a small horn, and a narrow pommel to allow a child to sit in front of its mother comfortably. The seat was made of quilted calfskin leather that is less slippery than a traditional seat, providing the riders with additional security. As with the brass-horned saddle, the mother and child saddle was not built for roping cattle, but was perfectly suitable for covering many miles and for performing basic cattle work. Though many women simply rode whatever saddle was available, for women of some means and for whom a saddle was an important part of their lives, there were a number of different styles on the market from which to choose and they were treated as prized possessions.[29] A note in the handwritten magazine *The Rocking P Gazette* suggests the value and significance of a woman's – or, in this case, a teenage girl's – saddle: "D. Macleay's saddle arrived from Riley and McCormick on May 9th. It was a dandy and the owner is now swelled up twice her usual size."[30] Possessing the correct working gear for the job was a matter of pride for women for whom working the range was both a requirement of their lifestyle and a source of identity and pleasure.

Over time and as they became more closely integrated into the working operations of their ranches, women dressed in a style that was uniquely western. The second generation of ranch women, those born and raised in the West, embraced clothing that was specifically suited to ranch life. As women adopted stock saddles and carried the same lariats as men, their "western" clothing took on a practical legitimacy of its own. Western dress

5.7 A TYPICAL WORKING OUTFIT BY THE 1930S. REPRODUCED WITH PERMISSION OF GLENBOW ARCHIVES.

grew increasingly appropriate for women to wear after the effects of World War I had loosened conventions of female propriety in society at large. This is when the classic image of the "cowgirl" that we recognize today was created. By the 1920s, ranch women, like their urban counterparts, were sporting short hair and shorter skirts. Few, if any, ranch women dressed as provocatively as the now ubiquitous, provocatively attired pin-up cowgirl. As illustrations in the early-1920s *Rocking P Gazette* indicate, wearing pants, breeches, or denim jeans for riding was by now standard practice, with modesty and practicality influencing fashion. Like their male counterparts, cowgirls and ranch women wore a range of items that were functional, stylish, or both. Moreover, women were proud of their cowgirl accoutrements.

Chaps, hats, boots, spurs, and ropes became essential components of women's working attire. The "matrimonial ads" that the teenage Macleay girls wrote in their magazine not only show a keen recognition of the practical desires of ranching men and women; they clearly reflect the sense of style that was typical of their time and place:

> A Wife might be welcomed by independent western cowboy from the East – She must be a first-class rider, roper, horse-judge and cow-milker – must appreciate western style of dress. Must

5.8 A NEW PAIR OF BOOTS WAS SOMETHING TO BE PROUD OF (1925). *ROCKING P GAZETTE*, COURTESY OF CLAY CHATTAWAY.

> have strongly developed bump of locality and be a trained guide in the foothills by day and night. Cowboy offers black Stetson, studded cuffaderos, and a wall-eyed horse.[31]

A hat, *vaquero*-style protective leather cuffs, and a horse were obviously seen as items valued both by working cowboys and by teenage ranch-raised girls.

By the time the frontier period was long over and ranching culture had been appropriated as entertainment in the form of rodeos and Wild West exhibitions, women were as likely as men to be seen decked out in full western costume. What had begun with practical adaptations to ranch life became a statement of equality, independence, and fashion. For the rodeo cowgirls who competed in the popular ladies' bucking events, trick riding, and races, their costumes were a source of pride and an expression of their individuality. These tenacious women wore colourful knee-high cowboy boots equipped with jingling spurs. They sported bloomers, leggings, and chaps in varying lengths, unique shirts and jackets specially designed to complement their pants, and a range of accessories such as scarves and belts. Of course, fundamental to their ensemble was an enormous wide-brimmed hat. Tad Lucas, a prominent American rodeo competitor in the

5.9 ADVENTURE AND A GREAT OUTFIT WERE ALL PART OF THE SHOW FOR COMPETITIVE RODEO COWGIRLS (1913). REPRODUCED WITH PERMISSION OF GLENBOW ARCHIVES.

1920s and 1930s, was famously photographed holding her infant daughter, Mitzi, comfortably nestled in her huge hat.[32] These women also unabashedly wore makeup and acknowledged that their beauty as well as their bravery impressed the crowds they entertained. Lucas recalled the importance of the costumes that she and her fellow competitors wore: "We all had lots of clothes. We always wore our best clothes, no matter what we were doing. If we had to ride a bull or a bucking horse or anything else, we wore our best clothes, we sure did."[33]

Rodeo cowgirls represented the extreme side of women's western fashion, but by the 1930s, on ranches everywhere, women wore clothes that reflected their lifestyle and occupation and enabled them to work freely and comfortably. The evolution of women's clothing in ranching communities reflected, and perhaps even encouraged, the increasing emancipation of women in society at large and manifested in apparel and equipment appropriate for the physical work they performed on the ranch alongside their male counterparts.

CHAPTER SIX

The Significance of Horses to Women's Emancipation

Horses were central to the lifestyle and livelihood of cattle ranchers and played an important role in dismantling constructions of gender roles in the West. A western icon, the horse was a means of transportation essential to the work, and recreation, of cowboys and ranchers. For women, riding and horses could be the ultimate gender equalizer. When mounted, a woman was as capable as her male counterpart. Pioneer rancher Agnes Morley Cleaveland reflected that "the cattle business in those days was conducted on horseback. Any rider who knew what to do was the equal of any other rider who knew what to do."[1] Unlike the farming districts that were densely settled by homesteaders after 1900, ranching districts remained sparsely inhabited by necessity.[2] Thus, women who did not ride were at a distinct disadvantage if they lived on a ranch. Without the ability, means, or desire to ride, a woman's mobility was limited, her opportunity for social contact with other women was severely reduced, and she was unable to partake in the primary mode of production – cattle work. Evidence from Alberta ranching country indicates that women who rode, with or without a practical purpose, used this modality for enjoyment, personal fulfilment, and social interaction. This was true for the second generation of ranch women as well. Women and girls with access to horses conveyed a sense of fulfilment and contentedness in their lives in spite of the isolation and hard work associated with ranch life. This chapter will demonstrate how the horse directly contributed to pioneer ranch women's ability to participate actively and equitably alongside their male counterparts.

In the male-dominated environment of the open-range period prior to 1900, women often were accepted and integrated into the ranching community through displaying their equestrian ability and being able to participate in the same working and recreational activities as the men. Riding was a valuable skill for ranch women to possess, whether they had come west as accomplished horsewomen or learned to ride upon their arrival. When Mary Ella Inderwick first arrived from eastern Canada as a bride, an informal initiation – often in the form of a riding evaluation – was a rite of passage for greenhorn women, as well as for men. In her correspondence to her sister in-law in the East, likely written with future publication in mind, Inderwick asserted that her high status among the men was due in part to her abilities as a rider and that she took pleasure in the freedom provided by their acceptance of her riding the open range. She wrote that the cowboys "back me in all my schemes because I ride well. . . . I verily believe that if I did not ride they would have nothing to do with me, [but] as it is they are rather proud of me."[3] Women often surprised the men with their abilities. Many women recalled the pride they had felt after their initial initiation into the ranks of the western cowboy. Violet Pearl Sykes, who was at the time a guest on a working ranch, recounted her debut at a roundup where she had been required to cut a specific steer out of a herd of a thousand. According to her memoirs, she had surpassed the men's expectations:

> Was I ever scared but I did not dare show it. Old Sammy was the perfect cut horse so into the herd of one thousand or more cattle I reined the old horse. . . . Sammy did all the work while I was riding for all I was worth. The herd hold boys were all watching to see how I made out which must have met with their approval and satisfaction because after that, they really put me to work whenever I went to the roundup.[4]

Evelyn Springett was also subjected to blatant scrutiny upon her arrival on the ranching frontier in 1893, and she was equally proud of herself for being immediately accepted as a suitable addition to the range. Her hazing consisted of being taken for a wild ride behind a team of fresh Hackney stallions by the manager of the Winder Horse Ranch on her first morning as a young bride out on the range. She recalled both the ride and the praise that followed it:

> To me it was a thrilling experience and one far more exciting than the fastest motor car. . . . Even though I was terrified I would not have missed the experience for anything. . . . My husband, watching it all, was furious with anxiety, but all Sharples [the manager] said on our return was "Why, man alive, your wife's all right; she'll do!" And from a Western man that was a high compliment.[5]

Most women were conscious of the fact that they had to prove their capabilities, and their spirit, to more experienced members of the ranching community, particularly to the cowboys who were the experts at working cattle and the supposed equestrian masters of the frontier. In addition, as scholar Nancy Young suggests, "the ability to connect with men both in task and conversation ('horse talk')" helped women to integrate socially into ranching communities.[6] Those who were competent riders and exhibited the willingness to participate in equestrian endeavours earned the respect of the men with whom they rode and, in short order, became accepted "hands" on the range.

The central role of the horse contributed significantly to the egalitarian nature of ranch work and to women's elevated status. Mounted, a woman was equal in strength and prowess to her male counterparts: she could gather cattle, help with sorting and cutting out stock, rope cattle for branding and medical treatment, wrangle horses, break colts, and perform virtually any other task that could be performed from the back of a horse. One Montana ranch woman, left to manage the place during the spring of 1886 while her husband was on a roundup, found that she was much more capable of getting the work done than their hired man. In a letter that was later published she related how she confidently handled the demands of a diverse range of daily activities:

> No sooner had he started than Van [the hired man] comes to me, and, in a coaxing tone of voice, persuades me to jump on my horse and drive in a bunch of mares for him. I had such a

> nice ride after them, and helped a man, whom I didn't know, to drive some cows, which he had found near our place, part of the way home. Then I drove our mares in, unsaddled my horse, and went at what Jem calls my "Fetish" *i.e.* house cleaning.[7]

On moderately sized ranches that functioned with minimal outside help, women took on duties that were performed by cowboys and hired hands on the larger outfits. Equipped with a horse and the desire to contribute to her family, a ranch woman extended her sphere of influence to encompass more than the house and the barnyard, and she enjoyed the status and sense of self-worth that accompanied riding the range.

Women participated in many, if not all, of the ranching activities performed on horseback, and in doing so, they broke out of traditionally separate, gendered labour roles. Riding enabled women to enter the masculine domain as an equal. Not only did women sustain their families by performing duties within the home, but they could work on horseback independently or alongside the men to accomplish necessary ranch work. Most ranches employed hired help year-round and even the smallest ranches tended to hire cowhands or haying crews when necessary. However, operations capable of meeting their labour needs without having to hire excessive outside labour were able to conserve scarce capital resources. Wives, daughters, and sisters who were capable horsewomen, knew the lay of the land well, and had a vested interest in the care of their stock were often better equipped to perform ranch work than employed cowboys. It was this direct contribution to the primary mode of production that elevated women's status on the range, and it was the central role of the horse that made this possible. While their skills made them indispensable to the productivity of their family units, women and girls who were considered "good hands" earned respect that extended well beyond their family circle. Dorothy and Maxine Macleay, for example, garnered admiration as a result of their contribution to their family's ranching success; they were also lifelong horsewomen. According to one of their contemporaries, "both girls were known throughout the ranching fraternity and broader as being very capable and talented young women."[8] Later, Dorothy's children were, like their mother, a fundamental asset to the ranch. They rode and performed any task that needed to be done. Accordingly, "this resulted in the girls as well as the boys becoming quite capable in the work involved in ranching."[9] Their father "often remarked that he would try to arrange some of the jobs for weekends because the kids were better help than most men that he could hire."[10] The second and third generations of ranch women were born into an environment made egalitarian by the horse.

While women often worked hard to develop the skills they needed to perform alongside the men, ranch children in general were simply raised in the saddle. For most boys and girls, riding was as natural and essential an activity as walking. Cleaveland affirmed this: "Horses were an integral part of our lives. The day's activity began no more by putting on one's clothes than by 'getting up the horses.'"[11] In fact, often before they could walk ranch children were placed on the front of a saddle, rocked to sleep by the swaying rhythm of a horse's gait and soothed by the creaking of the saddle. As they grew bigger, children would graduate to doubling or even tripling behind their parents or older siblings. Independence was gained by riding solo and maturity marked by participating in the real ranch work. Elizabeth Lane emphasized the significance of riding in her children's ranch upbringing. The family had a treasured "kids' horse" named McGuinty who was a valuable asset as an instructor to the next generation of ranch hands:

> All first six children learned to ride on him. The last learner rode behind the best rider until the day their father said he could ride alone and he was given the reins and told to go. When the children were allowed to join the older riders and McGuinty found himself with the other mounts he would snort and prance and make the children feel very proud of him. After they could ride with a sidesaddle or a stock saddle the children got other horses.[12]

A solid and trustworthy horse was invaluable as a first mount, but it was when a child graduated to a competent cow horse that they became truly integrated into the functioning of a working ranch. Lane remembered how important this step was for her children: "The great day came when a child was allowed to ride a well-trained cow pony whose quick turns and stops and swings from left to right was a test of riding."[13]

6.1 Horses were an essential part of growing up on the range (1912). Reproduced with permission of Glenbow Archives.

Ranch women's memoirs frequently reflect upon the nature of the relationship they had with their first horse – often a partner who was an indispensable, if sometimes infuriating, part of their early childhood. Acquiring her own horse made the ride to school more enjoyable for Carley Cooper: "I used to have to ride to school with my brother. We had two gates to open and he'd jump off to open the gates and when he jumped back onto the horse, sometimes he'd knock me off. I used to have to step on his foot, and he'd take my hand and pull me up and I'd sit behind him. When we got a little older I got a horse of my own and that was a lot nicer."[14] In an interview late in her life, Cochrane-area rancher Edna Copithorne laughingly remembered her first horse, a little black pony: "That was the only horse I ever hated. . . . [It] only had one gait and it was a slow one, oh I cried over that horse. . . . I soon ditched the old plugs and rode some smart ones to school."[15] Similarly, as children's horses were (and still are) notorious for outsmarting their riders, Constance Loree recalled the challenges of her first mount: "Daffy was a pretty, nice-gaited little pony but full of devilish tricks. He ran away with us, he rolled in rivers, he reared and bucked, and ran in and bit other horses' stomachs without missing a step. [My sister]

Mary and I loved him dearly, and rode him for years."[16] Providing children with mobility was a horse's fundamental role, and reliability was a trait more favourable than fancy bloodlines or pedigree. Millie Blache, who was born on her family's ranch on the Elbow River west of Calgary in 1896, had such a horse, "a pony which she rode to school named 'Monday' which was obtained in a trade with the Indians for 3 pounds sugar and 1 pound of tea."[17] These horses were children's partners in work and play and endowed them with mobility and responsibility at an early age.

Horsemanship skills were passed down generationally. Learning to ride and care for horses was fundamental to becoming a productive, responsible member of a ranching family and community. Daughters as well as sons were educated in the ways of the horse. Loree, a lifelong rancher, remembered her father's instruction in horsemanship as an integral part of her early childhood:

> He was a lenient father, putting up with our "tom-foolery" as he called it, but in matters of horsemanship the rules were strict and his word was law. Any infraction such as bringing a horse home winded and sweating, and his blue eyes could turn awfully cold, and you'd better have a good excuse. He had learned in a harsh school that survival could depend on not making a mistake, particularly in regard to the horse you were riding. If anything happened to it you were afoot and helpless. We were taught to ride safely and well, to ensure our welfare and the horse's. Riding was more than just sticking on and going fast. It was learning about the vulnerable parts of a horse: withers, back, stifle joint, mouth, and hooves, and how to prevent colic, founder, cinch gall, rope burn, and wire cuts.[18]

Loree's mother also provided the young equestrian with instruction, by reciting rhymes to encourage good horsemanship: "Your head and your heart keep bravely up,/ Your heels and your hands keep down,/ Your knees keep close to the horse's side/ And your elbows close to your own."[19] However, not all lessons came directly from a parent. Sometimes it was the animal itself that provided children with necessary instruction. Evelyn Cochrane wrote to her son about a visit she had made to a neighbouring ranch where she encountered a boy who had been "educated" by his horse:

6.2 Josephene Bedingfeld on a pony – note the child's unusual riding seat (c.1913). Reproduced with permission of Glenbow Archives.

"Poor little George has got a nasty sore place on his face, where the horse kicked him and broke his jaw. I believe he had been hitting the horse, for a stick was found lying beside him on the ground."[20] This incident was a cautionary tale. The fact that Cochrane chose to relate it to her son indicates the importance ranchers placed on teaching their children good horsemanship, not only for the practical purpose of protecting a valuable asset, but for developing and demonstrating decent moral character as well.

Mounted work enabled girls to transcend gender divisions and perform equitably alongside their male siblings and it also gave them the means to provide their families with supplementary income. Historian Elliot West's ground-breaking analysis of childhood on the frontier cites numerous examples of ranchers' daughters who "hired out" as herders for neighbouring farms and ranches. Stock work was the most common form of employment for range-raised children, he argues, and "among the young, the demands of the frontier ate away at distinctions of age and gender."[21] Provided one could ride, there was no shortage of work for youngsters of either sex. Claude Gardiner, an Alberta rancher, had neighbours with young daughters who broke and sold horses. In a letter written to his mother and his sister, Barbara, before their upcoming trip to the West, he wrote: "Can Bab ride yet? I shall get her a nice pony. I have no problem

6.3 Capable children made significant contributions on family ranches (1925). *Rocking P Gazette*, courtesy of Clay Chattaway.

with that as I know some people called Arnold who raise horses. They have several girls who ride and break horses and they can be trusted to have a good quiet one or two."[22] Whether they worked at home or were employed outside of the family, girls learned that they were valuable and productive members of their family units. And for girls, in particular, riding and a lifelong connection to horses assured them of an equitable position in ranching communities. It was this second generation of ranch women that most obviously benefited from the autonomy gained by riding for work and recreation.

Among the many hazards that could threaten a ranch's livestock was the danger of cattle becoming mired in bogs or muddy watering holes. Without prompt assistance, cattle would weaken while struggling to get out and often perish. On extensive tracts of grazing land, it was only by chance that someone would discover a bogged-down animal. Therefore, having children capable of riding the range and performing competently in an emergency was a major advantage. As the sketch above from the handwritten magazine *The Rocking P Gazette* indicates, women and girls who were skilled with a horse and rope were assets to the family ranch. The Macleay sisters used the *Gazette* to record their exploits on the ranch during the 1920s and in doing so provided insightful documentation of women's contributions to the family ranch. In this incident, the "staff" –

that is, the owner's daughters Dorothy and Maxine Macleay – are seen rescuing a cow with the aid of their governess.

The girls roped the animal around her head and front legs in order to drag her out, while the governess "tailed" the cow to encourage her to get up.[23] The community at large also benefited from women with expertise in handling a rope. The Morris sisters in the Pincher Creek district used their talents to assist their neighbours. As Nettie Smith, the daughter of homesteaders, recalls: "One day one of our cows ran into the lake to get away from the heel flies. We couldn't get her out to milk her. The Morris girls came riding through. They took down their lariats, rode out into the lake[,] lassooed the cow and drug her out. How I admired their skill!"[24]

In most households, it was one's age and accomplishments, rather than one's sex, that determined a person's status and responsibilities within the family. Boys and girls alike were given tasks that contributed to the family's livelihood and well-being. Even when some families attempted to maintain rigid barriers of gender differentiation, the equalizing factors of frontier existence – such as independence and practicality – usually acted to blur the lines between boys' and girls' activities. Agnes Mary Gibson was raised in such a family. Left to her own devices on the range with the same burden of responsibility to bear as her brothers, she adapted to the situation, which enabled her to perform as an equal despite the prohibitions on her behaviour:

> An only girl with six brothers, Agnes was something of a tomboy in spite of the efforts of her Victorian-minded parents. They were determined that she should ride sidesaddle like a lady, but since they had no proper saddle, she was expected to ride that way on a western stock saddle. To please them she would start out that way, but as soon as she was out of sight of the house, she was astride the horse like her brothers.[25]

Gibson later went on to become a very accomplished horsewoman, competing and excelling in riding, jumping, and driving events. Similarly, Cleaveland worked alongside her brother: "Although I rode sidesaddle like a lady, the double standard did not exist on the ranch. Up to the point of my actual physical limitations, I worked side by side with the men,

6.4 Horses provided fun and freedom (1922). Reproduced with permission of Glenbow Archives.

receiving the same praise or censure for like undertakings."[26] For Bessie Park MacEwan, who had been trained to ride at her family's stable in Scotland, moving to Alberta in 1906 gave her unprecedented freedom when her father conceded to the ways of the range: "At first I used Mother's side saddle, but one day Father weakened and brought home a lovely Australian saddle for me. Previously he had said it was unladylike for a girl to ride astride. I also rode a little racing saddle. I learned to break the odd horse and even broke a cow to ride (bareback)."[27] Girls took advantage of the freedom to work and play unsupervised and they, and their families, discovered that they were equal to the demands of the frontier.

By performing key jobs and routine chores on horseback at home, girls learned skills that enabled them to fulfil other ambitions, such as competing in horse shows and rodeos. Augusta Hoffman, whose family moved from the United States to ranch near Wood Mountain, Saskatchewan, in 1905, recalled that "at the age of thirteen I took over the job of mowing and raking the hay. . . . I was the one that did all the riding to look after the horses and cattle."[28] The same year that Hoffman took on greater responsibility on the ranch, she proudly earned her first dollar by riding in a ladies' horse race.[29] By the turn of the century, as communities and recreational activities became more organized, there were a number of riding events that women and girls could partake in. Ladies' races and relay races were common at local fairs. Women entered their own saddle horses or were offered mounts to test against one another to the delight of the crowds. In the public arena, women and girls proved themselves as talented performers, athletes, and riders alongside their male counterparts. Those who could ride, and ride well, earned status and recognition for their accomplishments.

Armed with equestrian ability and the spirit of the frontier, women obtained new-found independence and income by performing in rodeos and exhibitions. The widely popular and seminal western performance show "The Real Wild West," directed by Buffalo Bill Cody, represented women who had acquired their skills on working ranches. As Glenbow Museum curator Lorain Lounsberry writes, "Most of Cody's troupe was neither rich nor famous when they were hired – they were regular people who had skills you needed in the western cattle country."[30] Though the rodeo circuit was certainly not profitable for all, competitive riding was a viable way for women to earn a wage. Flores LaDue, perhaps the most famous Canadian performance cowgirl, used her income from trick roping and riding to help pay for the Alberta ranch she and her husband, Calgary Stampede founder Guy Weadick, purchased in 1920.[31] Though the adventurous, travelling career of a rodeo cowgirl was far removed from the realities of ranch women's daily existence, the public image they presented did accurately reflect the skills that many female ranchers possessed and the sense of independence that went with them. At larger shows and rodeos, women participated in races as well as roping competitions, trick riding, and even dangerous and once strictly male-dominated events such as bronc riding and steer wrestling. Cowgirl poet Jeanne Rhodes pays tribute to rodeo rider Fannie Sperry in a poem that depicts Sperry's transition from a hardworking ranch-raised young girl to a reputable performer to an independent business woman, and her lifetime of activities that centred around the horse:

> At an age when many children clutch a doll in either arm,
>
> Fannie Sperry captured mustangs that ran wild behind
> their farm.

Brought them home and broke and trained them, sold them to the folks around,

Who were sure that, trained by Fannie they were trust-worthy and sound.

First she rode at local horse shows where they passed the hat with pride,

Cuz she stayed with bucking horses that the cowboys couldn't ride;

Then she rode in ladies' relays, racing finest thorobred [*sic*] horses,

Changing mounts and even saddles as they sped around their courses . . .

Her reputation solid and her fame now spreading wide,

The budding sport of Rodeo sought her out to ride;

When Calgary, Alberta, had its first Stampede event,

The finest were invited and Fannie Sperry went . . .

For ten years Bill and Fannie toured their own Wild Western Show,

And then retired as outfitters – showed hunters where to go;

And when Bill died in '40, Fannie ran the business still,

For *steel* was in her spine long before she met old Bill.[32]

It was not until a series of fatal accidents combined with the economic pressures of World War II – which made it difficult for rodeo organizers to provide a men's and women's string of bucking stock – that women's bucking events were terminated.[33] Thanks to their horsemanship skills and their desire to test the boundaries of acceptable female behaviour, the

6.5 Performer Flores LaDue was skilled with a rope and a horse (c.1912). Reproduced with permission of Glenbow Archives.

indomitable women who partook in these events demonstrated to mass audiences that women of the range were equally as capable as the cowboys.

For most women on ranches, horses were an important tool of their work, but most fundamentally the horse provided women with mobility – and thus freedom. The expansiveness of the range made it imperative that women use horses as a means of transportation. Women learned the layout of the landscape from the back of a horse, confidently covering miles of open country at the reins of a wagon, democrat, or sleigh. Genuine horse-powered transportation was critical. Riding provided a means of escape from the solitude and isolation of ranch life. Whether it was riding to get the mail, travelling by wagon to the nearest centre for essential supplies, or riding to neighbouring ranches for social calls, women depended on the horse to keep them connected to their community. For, as Monica Hopkins noted, "a neighbour is anyone within a radius of 20 miles."[34] Even women who had no previous experience learned to ride and drive if

6.6 Popular schoolteacher Isabelle Lawson was gifted a horse and saddle by the community (1907). Reproduced with permission of Glenbow Archives.

they wished to have an independent means of travel. Hopkins did not even know what a democrat was upon her arrival in the West, only that it was an item her husband "deemed necessary now that there was to be a woman on the ranch."[35] As she soon learned, "the democrat turned out to be a cart on four wheels with two seats and I discovered we were going to use it right away as we intended to go home that day. . . . I felt somewhat as if I was sitting on the box seat of a carriage at home."[36] Not long after, Hopkins began to ride and drive on her own, exploring her new surroundings and becoming acquainted with the other women in the Priddis area.

The means and the ability to ride enabled women to actively engage with their peers and their community. Having access to horses and the opportunity to ride often made the difference between relishing the frontier experience or suffering from a sense of isolation and loneliness. In the late 1800s in New Mexico, Cleaveland, who ranched with her mother and siblings, witnessed the isolation endured by women who did not have a purpose to ride every day: "Not many of our woman neighbors got about as did my mother and her daughters. Not many had reason to, with their menfolks [*sic*] to carry on the responsibility of looking after their cattle. It was this deadly staying at home month in and month out, keeping a place of refuge ready for their men when they returned from their farings-forth, that called for the greater courage, I think."[37] After a visit with several women who had been driven to her ranch in a wagon by their husbands, Hopkins observed that "those who do not ride and are dependent on their men folk to take them about evidently do not get taken out very much; they seemed to think it was a great occasion. I've decided that I am not going to be dependent on anyone so I ride nearly every day, generally just around the place but I have been out on the range alone."[38] When women did not ride, it not only limited their mobility but severely restricted their means of entertainment. Inderwick, for whom transportation and recreation revolved primarily around horses, mused about a neighbour: "I often wonder how Miss Smith passes her time, having no household duties and not being a very ardent horse woman."[39] Women who did not ride were also not as easily integrated into ranch society. Both Evelyn Springett and Dorothy Blades acknowledged that the well-being of the governesses employed on their ranches was directly linked to their aptitude for horseback riding. Springett remembered one governess whom the children loved to tease, especially when on "horseback where she was both unhappy and insecure."[40] On the Rocking P Ranch, the Macleays went through a series of "school marms" before they found one who was suitable: an Englishwoman who liked horseback riding and stayed a long time.[41]

Evelyn Cochrane was one of many women who accepted the fact that they would have to ride and be flexible – and to adapt to any situation that may present itself – to maintain friendships. Her days on the CC Ranch west of Cayley were filled with riding. Cochrane's diary is a record of rides for cattle work, hunting, and business engagements, rides for routine chores such as fetching the mail and shopping, and frequent rides for the pure pleasure of exploring the range and making social calls. The incredible distance between ranches did not hamper her ability to make impromptu visits to keep in touch with the other women in the district. In a letter, she detailed her visits to three neighbouring ranches; each visit reveals pertinent information about the nature of frontier social calls via horseback. Travelling alone, save for the company of her dogs, Cochrane found her hostess at the first ranch occupied by washing, so, after a brief visit, she moved on. Arriving unannounced was standard range protocol and visitors were typically welcomed warmly. However, the visitor took the chance that her hostess may be preoccupied or may not even be home to welcome a weary traveller. For a confident horsewoman like Cochrane, the unpredictable nature of range travel was simply part of the experience. The next morning, following an overnight stay at the Oxley ranch, she found that her dogs had accompanied a passing wagon heading south for coal – "so I had to saddle up quickly and go after them. I caught them in about 4 or 5 miles, but it was all out of my way."[42] As she passed through Pine Coulee on her way to her next stop, the dogs killed a coyote; unexpected adventures required women to adapt to the situation at hand, particularly when travelling alone. Then it was on to the Norrish ranch to visit "Francey & Co." Cochrane wrote, "They have got a little pony to ride, and they quarrel all the time who is to ride it, and which saddle is to be put on. It seemed a long suffering creature. Francey is afraid herself to ride and yet does not like the others to get up."[43] Evidently, Francey Norrish had not yet been conditioned to the essential role of the horse in her own potential enjoyment of the frontier experience; thus, her mobility and her opportunity to socialize with other women were likely considerably more restricted than Cochrane's. Embracing the adventures that accompanied frontier experience went a long way in relieving women's boredom and encouraging their independence.

For all the freedoms and pleasures it afforded ranch women, travel was not without its hazards and hardships. Women had to have confidence to travel through remote cattle country. Inhospitable terrain, weather conditions, wildlife, and unpredictable range cattle all presented challenges. During the open-range period in particular, feral cattle were among the most dangerous things a traveller could meet. Gladys Baptie recalled an encounter with a gathered herd of cattle: "I remember one day my mother, sister and I went to [the town of] Cochrane with a one horse buggy and six riders escorted us thru' the cattle, as the big steers would have attacked us."[44] Having children limited women's mobility and created additional worry when travelling. Hester Jane Robinson remembered the "lonely life" she and her children spent on the ranch near Bragg Creek, Alberta, while her husband rode the range moving cattle for his father. On the return trip from a rare visit with a neighbour across the river, Robinson's baby daughter was thrown from the wagon and almost drowned.

> Mother let the baby drop into the river – luckily up stream, and as Kathleen floated under the democrat she washed up against one wheel. Joe, with great presence of mind and taking a long grip on the reins, grasped Kathleen's long clothes still maintaining control of the colts. I calmed myself with a half glass of brandy, then nursed the baby and she slept for 12 hours![45]

Many ranch women faced this dilemma: staying at home meant enduring isolation, while travelling could mean putting themselves and their children at risk.

Women raised in the West were often more comfortable travelling in remote areas than those who were recent arrivals. Growing up on the cattle frontier had prepared Violet Pearl Sykes for negotiating the multiple challenges associated with range travel. Her confidence and skill with a horse meant she was capable of overcoming the obstacles associated with seemingly simple routines, such as getting the mail:

> I was more or less elected to ride up there [the NWMP Barracks] to see if there was mail. The distance from the ranch to the barracks was ten miles over the bench top. By going over the bench top one did not have to ford the river twice nor open the wire gates[,] which was a real effort for a girl. There were so many dead cattle from the hard winter that I found them very useful in helping me find my way about the prairies. At the fork of the road there was a dead Texas steer with huge horns and that was my sign to turn to the river bottom on the trail that led to the police camp.[46]

Tenacious women were entrusted with jobs that gave them mobility and adventure. One of these women was Sykes; another was Lucy Seymour of Claresholm, who recalled wild driving experiences. Seymour's husband broke teams of work horses to supplement the family's livelihood on the ranch. He would start the colts in June and then send her to town with them pulling a wagon by mid-summer. Once the horses were quiet, they would be put to work on threshing operations in the fall. Laughingly, Seymour admitted that the horses would usually buck most of the way to town – an occurrence that obviously did not faze her.[47] Women adapted to the circumstances of ranch country by learning how to ride, drive, and handle horses under frontier conditions with confidence, and these skills diminished their sense of isolation and the helplessness associated with immobility.

Even after the advent of motorized vehicles – which began to share the range with horses around 1910 – horses remained a vital mode of transportation in ranching country.[48] Transportation by horseback was simply better suited to the conditions of travel, particularly in the foothills ranching districts. The earliest cars were not hardy enough to access many remote ranches and rural road conditions were impassable by vehicle much of the time. When Catherine Bond Dick began ranching with her husband on Willow Creek in 1914 they used a four-horse team to travel to High River twice a year for a "grub stake." She recalled that "later we had a car and then it was we wished for better roads, fewer, gates and no mud holes."[49] Progress in the form of technology did not suit pioneer rancher Bob Newbolt. In his memoirs he reflects with hostility on the "intrusion" of farmers into ranching country – and also curses his motor car. He would run it right through farmers' fences and gates if they were in the way of the trail; often the "bally" car got stuck in the mud. Newbolt divulged that his wife "soon learned to take along her tatting or knitting; she would have something to occupy her time while I walked to get someone to pull my motor car out of a mud hole."[50] Constance Loree recalled that, in the 1920s, "even the [twelve-mile] drive from Nanton to the ranch was an adventure with those early cars that overheated on steep grades. The road was graded as far as William's Coulee [five miles]. After that it was little more than a broad trail which angled off to the left past the old buffalo jump and up through the hills, with wire gates to open. It was impassable in wet weather."[51] Like other ranch women, Loree and her mother and sister used horses as their primary mode of transportation between the "homeplace" and their summer ranches in the Porcupine Hills, even if it entailed some challenges:

> Mary and I carried some strange burdens on those rides. Once it was the bread dough, which wasn't quite ready for the oven, another time a kettle of citron marmalade carried between us on a broom handle. One late fall exodus from the ranch involved

> two very large cats, each stuffed in a flour sack, squalling and spitting. How the horses hated that! We decided that there was one advantage to riding a wild horse – you didn't have to carry as much.[52]

When one's business was cattle and horses it made sense to use genuine horsepower for most necessary travel. The guest book from Trail's End Ranch indicates that, as late as the 1930s, much of the travel to and from the ranch was done on horses – and clearly with good reason:

> May 23rd D.C.I. on horseback, found the longest way round was *not* the shortest way home. . . . July 5th F.W. Ings bad journey down. Had to leave car in the mud. . . . Oct. 11th Came up to move cattle Constance and E.H.I. on Slick and Pilot. . . . Oct. 20th Gathered cattle at Sunset & cut out calves for weaning. . . . Oct. 31st Constance E.H.I. Kelly brought up 12 heifers to Sunset & 1 D K heifer took in the calves that had broken out of the weaning pen. Travelled the old trail & lunched on a lichen covered rock . . . ginger bread & apples.[53]

Practical, versatile, and enjoyable, horses were an integral part of ranch operations long after vehicles were in use.

Just as they contributed to women's engagement in their working communities and facilitated the mobility necessary for creating networks of social support, horses were central to the recreation and social activities of early ranchers. From imported pastimes such as polo, racing, and hunting with hounds to informal pursuits like camping and picnicking, the horse facilitated much of the recreation in fledgling ranching communities. The presence of equestrian sports on the frontier created a familiar social atmosphere for ranchers of British and Eastern Canadian origins, many of whom were already entrenched in an equestrian culture. Polo matches and horse races were important and well-attended social events. Even Monica Hopkins, who as the daughter of a clergyman would never have attended the races in England, looked forward to the Millarville Races – "the chief social event of the year out here."[54] Horse sports had a levelling effect on the frontier. Whereas in England and the East many horse sports were accessible only to the upper classes, thanks to the surplus of inexpensive horses on the frontier "even quite poor people could now indulge in the tastes of gentlemen."[55] Women were active participants in all equestrian activities. In the ranching district immediately west of Calgary, the Blache sisters were known for their equestrian pursuits: "Fox hunts and paper chases were two of the exciting sports enjoyed by Beatrice and Millie. They were both excellent horsewomen and would ride side-saddle over the paper chase course. It was a cross country race laid out by bits of paper which were to be followed over the course jumping over fences, creeks, brush, and other obstacles."[56] There is evidence that from their earliest arrival, in the 1880s, women rode out with the men to pursue coyotes or wolves. Some women garnered reputations as particularly skilled and daring riders, much appreciated by the men in their company. In his memoirs, pioneer rancher Fred Ings extolled the abilities of his neighbour Evelyn Cochrane:

> Some of the ladies in the country were keen coyote hunters, but none could imitate Mrs. Billy [*sic*] Cochrane. She had ridden to hounds in England with the Quorn pack, and was a good horsewoman and a fearless one. She always rode an outstanding horse. . . . How she was able to mount as she did, without help on a side saddle was a puzzle, but she could, and this Fox horse stood nearly sixteen hands high. She seemed to spring into that saddle with perfect ease, and once she was away, with her light weight, there were few of us who could keep up with her.[57]

Ranchers tested themselves and their horses against one another in equestrian competitions. Jumping events, horse shows, and gymkhanas were as common as rodeo in fledgling communities. Ings remarked that "though the horses for our cow work were trained for roping and such, we still liked to have them jump and perform, according to more civilized standards."[58] Women excelled in these competitions and competed against the men. Whether they showed horses for their conformation and breeding potential (like Mabel Newbolt, who was instrumental in importing high-calibre show horses) or they rode for sport (like Minnie Gardner, who awed the crowds with her bravery, jumping horses to daring heights), women were

6.7 Minnie Gardner jumping side-saddle to impressive heights (c.1900–03). Reproduced with permission of Glenbow Archives.

critical in creating and maintaining a recreational horse culture in ranching communities.

Women also used horses for informal pursuits such as exploring the wilderness that surrounded frontier ranches. Writing of children and horses on the frontier, Elliot West suggests that not only did horses provide children with companionship, entertainment, and mobility, but "horses expanded their opportunities to push out into the land; wild and tame creatures were part of the landscape that excited their curiosity."[59] One ranch-raised child who, like many of his contemporaries, attended school in the nearest town during the winter months wrote of the strong pull of the horses and the hills: "We never learned to swim or play tennis, because we headed for the hills and those cow ponies as soon as the end of June came."[60] Women, similarly curious and excited by the landscape, turned to horses as their means to engage with the wild. In Montana, Isabel Randall used her capabilities as a horsewoman to treat a less mobile friend to a holiday: "I brought Mrs. B— home with me to stay a few days, to have a little rest, which she much needed. She stayed with us about a week, and, when my work was done, I drove her about in the buggy; we went on some most beautiful drives, either up in the mountains or down

6.8 Horses provided transportation for social events, like berry picking (c. early 1900s). Reproduced with permission of Glenbow Archives.

by the river."[61] Hopkins and her friends camped in their free time. Riding and leading pack horses, they were able to trek deep into the mountains for days at a time. Their rustic adventures included fording rivers, fishing, and traversing steep trails.[62] Not all outings were that adventurous, but they were equally pleasurable. The use of horses enabled day trips into the foothills for picnics. Community outings would see the rough trails into the hills lined with democrats, wagons, and riders.[63] Horses were also used to gain access to the much-sought-after wild berries. Berries were an important part of the pioneer diet and women used berry picking as an excuse for a purposeful visit. While her family saved the berries closest to the ranch house for their visitors who did not ride, Constance Loree recalled how her mother had taught her daughters how their horses could help them to reach the best berries, which grew on the topmost boughs:

> Mary and I got very bored picking berries except for saskatoons, which often grew on such high bushes that we could stand on our saddles and strip the berries off in handfuls. . . . Poor Mother always wore her English riding boots, which had slippery soles. So often she would just get her pail filled, and she'd slip

> and fall. All that work for nothing! It wasn't easy carrying two pails of berries home on horseback. We usually sat in a handful of them and the saddles were stained purple. A lot of work went into a winter's supply of jam and preserves.[64]

Women's exploits were made easier by their ability to ride. They enjoyed the freedom to socialize and to explore the wilderness that served as their backyards.

On top of providing women with the ability to contribute and participate as equals in ranch activities, equipping them with the independence and gratification of mobility and serving as a form of recreation, the horse brought deep pleasure and comfort to many women through both its intrinsic nature and the practice of riding. Mary Inderwick wrote, "I do believe I could take pleasure in riding if I were a deaf mute. . . . If you could only feel the rocking motion of a good lope through the grass and hear the creak of the saddle, and see the horse's fresh look after a long ride at this pace."[65] Women used riding as a release from their everyday burdens and an escape from their sometimes stifling domestic duties. Edith Ings fostered in her daughters a love of horses that extended beyond their work on the ranch:

> For Mother there could never be enough riding. Even if she was tired after a day's housework, a ride would restore her like nothing else. Bad weather didn't deter her; she loved riding in the wind and rain and could stand cold better than anyone. She was the ringleader in our adventures, and sometimes we found her a bit daunting. Mary and I might be asleep in our beds and be jolted awake by Mother's "Girls! Girls! Get up! It's a perfect night for a ride." . . . Her horse was usually fast and frisky, and we had a time to keep up to her. She wasn't the type of mother who said "Now children, be careful." It was more like "here's a flat place. Let's gallop!"[66]

Women used horses to explore their territory and make themselves familiar with their home range, developing a sense of place and comfort in their new environment. Inderwick described her own horseback explorations:

"Often, I ride alone and then I see such wonderful things. I come suddenly on a small pond with ducks, a pond I must have been the discoverer of, as no one knew of it and all wanted to see it. But I have absolutely no bump of locality and I never could find it again."[67] Newly married Catherine Bond Dick similarly learned to feel at home on her ranch through the miles she spent in the saddle: "It was the most beautiful country I had ever seen, 'God's Country,' and it suited me exactly. . . . Ward said, 'Whenever I saddle up to go anywhere, you come too.' . . . So that was what I did, and by fall I knew every coulee, drift fence, creek, and spring on our big range."[68]

One of the most common reflections in ranch women's memoirs and personal histories is the significance of the horse in their lives. Rancher and rodeo cowgirl Fannie Sperry spoke of horses as the most important influence in her life, a sentiment shared by many ranch women: "I was born March 27, 1887 on a horse ranch at the foot of Bear Tooth Mountain north of Helena, Montana, and if there is a horse in the zodiac then I am sure I must have been born under its sign, for the horse has shaped and determined my whole way of life."[69] It was the intangible pleasures associated with the horse that provided so many women with enjoyment and instilled in them an intense appreciation for the ranching lifestyle and western environment. According to Lewis Thomas, who was raised in a pioneer ranching community in the Alberta foothills, "the horse was the divinity of a special cult."[70] Fortunately, this "cult" was open to members of both sexes, all of whom, out of necessity and an intrinsic love of the horse, centred their livelihoods and the majority of their social activities on horses. The horse – whether providing a means to participate equitably on working ranches, the responsibility to be a productive member of a family ranch and the community at large, the freedom of mobility on isolated ranges, or the simple pleasure of a gallop across open range – defined a way of life for early ranch women. Horses and the physical and psychological freedom they provided on the frontier enabled women both to overcome gender barriers and to participate as equals in the development of ranching communities.

Conclusion: At Home on the Range

This book has demonstrated the vital role of women in establishing enduring family ranches. From the earliest days of the cattle industry in southern Alberta, women played a fundamental role in managing cattle herds, maintaining homes, and rearing the next generation of ranchers. Many women were empowered by the hard work that was required of them and became engaged with primary production in addition to subsistence and domestic work. These women's status within their families and within society at large improved as they resourcefully met the challenges of frontier existence. Most ranch women proved that they were indeed as capable and confident on the frontier as were ranch men. However, not all women had the advantage of a true and equal partner. Some bore the bulk of the burden that surviving on a working ranch entails and endured the limitations of a patriarchal system of agriculture that enabled men to abuse their position of power within the family economy. The ranching lifestyle that promoted women's emancipation was the same one that could prove proscriptive. The physical and psychological demands of a life built in the foothills and on the prairies were transformative to individuals and helped to shape the society that emerged in ranching communities.

Men, as often as women, were confronted by the dismantling of their own gendered identities as preconceived expectations met pioneering reality. Whether as a liminal space or as a physical borderland between civilization and a landscape laden with untapped resources, the late-nineteenth- and early-twentieth-century conception of the frontier was intertwined with the construct of masculinity. Colonialism and the literature and public policy that promoted pioneer agriculture in the West relied on the notion that the frontier was a place where virility and strength were rewarded – and expected. Pioneer men brought with them to the West the anticipation of adventure and the promise of advancement. When those aims were challenged by the hardships and rough realties of ranching in an unknown environment, not only was a man's livelihood threatened, but his masculinity as well. The gendered expectation that a man ought to be the sole provider and protector of his family evolved as women became more than "helpmates" and instead became partners on family ranches.

While the constructs of masculinity and femininity were continually undermined by the realities of frontier existence, some men and women sought to uphold traditional gender distinctions as a way to maintain stability and normalcy in a life where daily existence was often fraught with challenges and uncertainty. Not all women were comfortable performing work that stretched beyond the boundaries of the domestic sphere. When there was essential work to be done, every member of the family was expected to contribute, but that did not necessarily mean preconceptions of a gendered division of labour were dismantled. Sometimes the desire to maintain separate spheres came from women themselves. These pioneer women recognized they were required to perform "men's work" but didn't thrive on it. When Sarah Roberts was expected to brand calves on her family's operation, for instance, she performed out of duty, not because she relished the chance to break out of her traditional gender role as so many others did. She wrote, "I stayed with my job until it was done, and I am glad that I never had to do it again. I think that it is not a woman's work except that it is everyone's work to do the thing he [or she] needs to do."[1] As this book has illustrated, while women's lifestyles on the ranching frontier were similar, their responses, reactions, and interpretations of their experiences were diverse. Despite this complexity, as scholar Jeanne Kay concludes, "most women were committed to survival, improvement of their lot as possible, sustaining family and friends, and their own sense of self in relation to a new and sometimes overpowering landscape."[2] Examining how women engaged with the natural environment brings a fitting conclusion to an analysis of a livelihood and lifestyle that was rooted in the land.

While pioneering men were more likely to use their work and their relationship to the economic order to understand their role in the ranching West, women seemed to understand themselves not only in relation to their labour, but in connection to the land itself. Reflections on the landscape emerged as a resoundingly common theme in ranch women's writings and reminiscences. An intimate relationship with nature empowered women physically and spiritually in the ranchers' West. An appreciation of their solitude and surroundings enabled ranch women not only to survive but to thrive in the rugged and isolated atmosphere of the ranching frontier. Much has been made of the loneliness suffered by pioneering women, and certainly, many of their memoirs attest to the trials of living without the companionship of other women or the security of established communities. However, my research confirms what anthropologist John W. Bennett noted in his study of agrarian societies on the northern plains: that "on the whole, the pioneers who came out West to ranch either valued isolation or were not particularly frightened by it."[3] According to their own words and as demonstrated by their actions, women readily adapted to the ranching frontier and embraced the lifestyle with little complaint. This book has discussed reasons for this, including a family economy that fostered an individual's independence and an egalitarian family environment, and the ready access to horses, which enabled mobility and a sense of personal freedom. It was a combination of these advantages that inured women to their remote ranching lifestyle. However, perhaps even more fundamentally and at an intrinsic level, it was their relationship to nature that most captivated women's imaginations and connected them to a sense of place and home in the West.

An attachment to their home range fortified women against the burdens of ranch life, such as isolation, uncomfortable living conditions, and the demands of domestic and physical labour, and this attachment increased their commitment to the success of their ranching enterprise. For some, this connection to place was immediate, while others grew accustomed to the landscape over time. Many women who came to know the northern ranges as adults definitively illustrate how their love of the land enabled them to overlook the challenging aspects of their pioneer experiences. Mabel Newbolt, who had agreed to marry her rancher husband on the condition that they remain on the ranch for only five years, soon became so attached to the place that, as her husband wrote, "before the five year period expired, Mabel was more in love with Bowchase [their ranch] and its beautiful surroundings than she seemed to be with her bally husband."[4] Agnes Skrine's writing contradicts an assumption that a ranch woman was "an object of pity" and considered "a household drudge." From her own experience on the Bar S Ranch west of Nanton in the 1890s, she argued that despite the obligatory housework and the presumed "want of congenial society," the opportunities for freedom and adventure afforded by the lifestyle enabled women to find fulfilment on the range.[5] The landscape dominated the content of Skrine's argument (which she published using the pseudonym Moira O'Neil). She described the joys of riding out across the hills, the impressive winds, the multitude of flowers, and the general grandeur of the vistas. The "out-of-door life here," she asserted, was what brought joy and satisfaction to the ranching community:

> I like the simplicity, the informality of the life, the long hours in the open air. I like the endless riding over the endless prairie, the winds sweeping the grass, the great silent sunshine, the vast skies, and the splendid line of the Rockies, guarding the west. I like the herds of cattle feeding among the foothills, moving slowly from water to water; and the bands of horses travelling their own way, free of the prairie. . . . I like the summer and the winter, the monotony and the change. Besides, I like a flannel shirt and liberty.[6]

The landscape and lifestyle of cattle country in southern Alberta, and their accompanying aesthetic and athletic pleasures, captivated women and encouraged their attachment to their own particular place on the prairie.

A sense of adventure combined with an appreciation for nature fostered in women a deep and enduring connection to their ranches. As Evelyn Springett wrote of her home on the New Oxley Ranch, "the air was so fine and clear . . . one felt a deep joy in just being alive and alone."[7] Like Springett, other women expressed a specific affinity for their home range. When Agnes Morley Cleaveland first glimpsed the panorama of her mother's newly acquired ranch in the wilderness of New Mexico, she was instantly awed by and attached to the landscape. She wrote, "I had no words at all. I was taking that scene into my heart and soul as *my country* for so long as I should live."[8] Exploring the landscape and learning the names of the local flora and fauna helped make women feel at home in their environment. These women, often with the company of their children, spent hours simply getting to know the lay of the land and becoming familiar with landmarks that oriented them on their ranches and in the region. Upon her arrival to their spread west of Stavely in 1919, Mary Streeter used the free time she had while her house was being built to become acquainted with her surroundings; she and her sons "roamed the hills and along the creeks, soon really loving the ranch."[9] The strangeness of the prairie and foothills were overcome by women who proactively sought to understand their new environments. After emigrating to the West from Nova Scotia, Catherine Bond's mother actively set out to identify unfamiliar plant species:

> One of the very worthwhile things that Mother did when we were all new to the West was to collect specimens of wild flowers – flower, leaf, seed, and root. These she would send to the Experimental Farm to be classified and the correct plant name would be sent to her. In that way we children were given an awareness of the plant life around us and the correct names of so many of our Alberta flowers.[10]

The sense of adventure that inspired women's explorations had multiple benefits. Their familiarity with local geography and native vegetation had practical applications for agriculture, while their understanding of the surroundings facilitated women's sense of place and belonging in the West.

Naming their ranches, or significant geographic points, also gave women a sense of connection to their immediate surroundings. Some, like Bob Newbolt's mother, who lived on her son's Alberta ranch from 1885 to 1891, embraced both the familiarity and the newness of the landscape. The name she gave the ranch reflected the integration of her cultural heritage with the specific resonance of her adopted home.

> She was happy and contented and took great interest in the ranch operations. She was especially fond of the tree covered

> flat below the ranch house along the river. It reminded her of similar scenes in England often referred to as a Chase. She added the name of the river, "Bow" to the former, making one word "Bowchase" and from that time on my ranch was known as "Bowchase Ranch."[11]

Encouraged by her mother, whose "wonder and delight in nature and the beauty of the hills was a celebration of life," my own grandmother Constance Ings Loree recalled a childhood rich with interactions that connected the family to their home:

> The sound accompaniment of those years is hoof beats. It was bliss to have all that beautiful country for our playground. We explored every corner of Sunset [Ranch], giving our own names to significant spots. We each had a mountain: two little hills, side by side. Mary Ings Mountain was steeper, but Conna Ings Mountain was bigger.[12]

Just as exploring and naming the land contributed to women's sense of belonging, active involvement in ranch work encouraged their attachment to place and solidified their role on the range alongside their male counterparts. This book has detailed women's various roles on family ranches and the multiple ways in which physical, productive efforts transformed gender roles within the family. Women and men baked bread, tended gardens, milked cows, broke horses, and worked cattle on the open range. This work that extended outside of the home and yard transformed how women perceived the physical environment. At a hearing concerning the proposal of Grasslands National Park – which now adjoins her family's ranch in southern Saskatchewan – Marjorie Linthicum expressed a commitment to the natural environment that had developed over a lifetime of ranching: "I have a special feeling for this land. . . . I appreciate and respect – first flowers in spring, the wide starlit sky and the night winds whistling, . . . the vastness of the prairie under a blanket of snow, the threat of an approaching snow storm and the shelter of a brush coulee. . . . I am as much a part of this land as the coyotes and the gophers."[13] Linthicum continued to explain that the depth of her familiarity with the landscape had been fostered by years of working on and with the land as part of a productive family unit. She expressed a sentiment found in most ranch women's writings: the significance of belonging to and working in a beloved place.

> I know what it's like to ride all day and never encounter another person, to have a faithful horse bring me home through a blinding storm, to drive cattle home in the fall and have them strung out for two or three miles heading for winter pastures, . . . to drive cows and calves to summer pastures and then sit and watch them mother up, to dream as a young girl of riding south to the Badlands and driving cattle with my dad and then having this dream come true.[14]

The egalitarian nature of ranch work, combined with the obligation to be out in the elements and engaged with the environment, fostered in many women not only a sense of commitment to their land and animals but a confidence in their own physical abilities and a transcendent sense of self.

Work and the physicality of ranching were not the only factors that shaped women's responses to their environment or defined their lives in the West. Their connection to the land enabled a spirituality that brought comfort, inspiration, and faith despite the paucity of churches on the frontier. American writer and rancher Gretel Ehrlich believes that, for many, the expansive geography of the grasslands possessed a healing power; "space has a spiritual equivalent and can heal what is divided and burdensome within us."[15] Many ranchers were educated women from the East, schooled in the classical Romantic tradition of art and literature that associated an experience of sublime beauty in nature with the power of a divine being. Thus, some women's response to their physical environment incorporated a mixture of aesthetics and spiritualism. Evelyn Springett described how the geography and weather of the foothills of the eastern slopes challenged her endurance but ultimately brought her peace:

> I wish I could give some adequate idea of the vast loneliness of my life on the prairie. All around us there was the never-ending roll of the hills, like huge sea waves, some of them mountains high. . . . Always and ever the feel of these Everlasting Hills was with us, and to them we looked for any change in the weather.

> Many and many a time, after a long spell of bitter cold, have I stepped out on to the freezing prairie to "lift up mine eyes unto the hills" from whence seemed to come our help, and under my frozen breath I have murmured the words, "Our help cometh from the Lord."[16]

Many ranch women developed such an essential connection to their environment that nature formed the basis of their spiritual beliefs.

Mary Inderwick, too, described a spiritual reaction when reflecting on the solace provided by the views on her ranch. In her isolation, she personified the mountains as companions, giving them more regard than "the bothersome humans" she occasionally encountered: "I have any number of troubles, in fact too numerous to mention, but I forget them all in this joyous air with the grand protecting mountains always standing round the western horizon. They seem the very spirit of the old hymn 'Abide with me – Oh Thou that changest not' – and they are the dearest most constant of friends."[17] The hills, the mountains, and the wind were the environmental features most frequently depicted in women's writing. Skrine described the effects of the infamous chinook winds and lyrically depicted the vista of hills and mountains from her ranch home in divine terms: "You may see to the west a whole range of the Rockies, magnificent, exultant – based on earth and piled against the sky like mountain altars, the snow-smoke rising from their dazzling slopes and melting away in the blue, as if the reek of some mighty sacrifice purer than human were ascending on high."[18] She, like so many other ranch women, found that engaging with the environment elevated her connection to the land. The ranchlands provided more than a means of making a living; they were solace from isolation, a source of spirituality, and ultimately a home.

This book has established that women have been at the core of the ranching industry for generations; from the earliest days to the present, they were essential to sustaining viable ranches and homes on the range. Ehrlich affirms that, for ranchers,

> being "at home on the range" is a matter of vigor, self-reliance, and common sense. A person's life is not a series of dramatic events for which he or she is applauded or exiled but a slow accumulation of days, seasons, years, fleshed out by the generational

> weight of one's family and anchored by a land-bound sense of place.[19]

I feel this "weight" myself, but there is no other burden I would want to carry. My hope is that in the routine of my days, which I spend preoccupied with the same concerns as those of my grandmother and great-grandmother – family and cattle – I can instill in my own children a sense of the responsibility that is entangled with our commitment to this land that we have called our own for a mere five generations. For the first women who took on the tasks of raising cattle and families in the West, work offered previously unknown opportunities. As their resourcefulness, status, and independence increased, so did their sense of belonging in the western grasslands. It is this belonging that is perhaps their greatest gift to their descendants. The second and subsequent generations have inherited a deep love of the natural environment and the ranching lifestyle. Today, women are increasingly taking over the management of ranches that have been in their families for years. Vernice Wearmouth, of the Wineglass Ranch near Cochrane, asserts that it is the connection to nature that motivates her daughter Edith, the current operator of the ranch, and her granddaughter to continue their family's legacy: "I think there's been four generations of women, and I wouldn't be surprised if she's the fifth to own this ranch and work on it. I think it's just the love of the outdoors and being able to get out with nature and the outdoor freedom."[20] Although modernization has changed some of the practices of ranching, it remains an industry to which women's contributions are as vital as men's. This analysis of frontier ranch women illustrates that ranching is, at its heart, a way of life largely sustained by families who are committed to working with the land – and with one another.

By initiating this project, I accepted Sarah Carter's scholarly challenge: that "in the Canadian West, serious and sustained study of women and the cattle industry remains to be done."[21] In these pages I have done my best to illuminate worthy lives, give voice to the stories waiting on browned and weathered pages, and illustrate the varied roles of women on the cattle frontier. However, the discussion of pioneer ranching women is far from complete. Indeed, I believe the conversation has just begun to get interesting. In Alberta, cattle culture has wide-reaching social and economic implications as well as deep roots that are intertwined with family history and personal memory. This particular assessment of ranching families is sure to stimulate reflections and incite further challenges. I hope this book acts as a catalyst for further study and that subsequent scholars will pick over the ideas presented here to tease out further complexities and re-evaluate and deepen my examination of our pioneers, all the while continuing to explore the connections of women to industry, family, and place in the cattle country of the Canadian West.

Appendix: "My Sunset Childhood" by Constance Ings Loree[1]

In 1919, some years after buying the Midway, our farm near Nanton, Dad acquired three thousand acres of grazing land in the Sunset District. One parcel was the Granville Heare land, later known as Trail's End. North and west was the Lake Section, so named because of its fair sized lake; the other parcel was the Sunset Ranch, where we had a summer home, and began our lifelong love affair with the foothills. The happiest times our family ever spent together were at Sunset. The memory of the years we spent there is so vivid that I feel if I could step back through the looking glass it would be just as it was, with the four of us together again.

There was an enchantment about our life there which we all felt. When I asked Mary recently "What can I write about Sunset? What was there about it?" she replied "It was because Mother made each day seem like a fairy tale." Her wonder and delight in nature and the beauty of the hills was a celebration of life. The miracle of the first crocus in spring, and the profusion of wild flowers that followed as the season advanced, the evening light of the crows against the sunset, storms, rainbows, first star and new moon all received her homage. Each day brought a new prospect of surprise and adventure.

The house, where I was born, stood in a valley just a quarter mile north of Sunset School. It was a plain little house covered with cedar shingles in a beautiful pattern, with a small porch front and back where we watched

A.1 Sunset Ranch west of Nanton, Alberta, was the Ings family's summer home (c.1920). Courtesy of Loree family.

sunrises and sunsets. It had a beautiful view of the mountains. Inside there was an entry-pantry, large kitchen with traditional cabinet and wood range, a small unplumbed washroom, three bedrooms, and a sitting room with wood heater. It was sunny and cozy and very welcoming. What a refuge it seemed at night, when the coal oil lamps kept the darkness at bay and our parents [were] there to ward off ghosts and goblins. Sometimes the dog would growl and bristle when coyotes howled, or an owl hooted outside the window, but we knew we were safe. The fragrance of willow burning, Mother's crocks of wine ripening, gooseberry jam simmering on the stove, rose petals drying for sachet, Dad's pipe, and the honest smell of horse and leather combined to give our house its special aroma. It was then that we appreciated the good books supplied by our grandparents in London, Ontario. Mother's hands were usually busy with a bit of sewing, or picking over the day's berries. Dad quite often would sit quietly, deep in his thoughts, and then he'd give a chuckle and say "Missus, did I ever tell you about the time . . ." And we knew we were going to hear one of his marvellous "yarns" from his rich store of memory.

Sometimes fierce storms would beat against the house, pounding rain and awesome flashes of lightening. With the first thunderclap I would be in Dad's lap. His chair was a wicker lounge, and he had attached telephone insulators to all six legs to make it lightening proof. Mother and Mary quite enjoyed storms and might go to the door to enjoy the show, saying "Oh, come and watch. It's beautiful!" But Dad and I would ride out the storm in his magic chair, for he was nearly as afraid of thunderstorms as I was. He'd had his share of being out on the range behind a herd of cattle with no shelter. During one particularly awful thunderstorm when I was limp with fear he said, "Never mind. It's too bad to last." It seemed like cold comfort.

Dad's frontier days had left habits he found hard to break. By the time Mary and I came along, Mother had persuaded him not to sleep with his six shooter under the pillow; it now hung in the cartridge belt on the bed post, or on the back of the chair. But it was always at hand. It bothered him to sit in a room that was lit up at night unless the blinds were down, and he would go out of his way to avoid walking between a lamp and the window. He didn't lack courage, but he didn't believe in making himself a target.

He was a lenient father, putting up with our "tom-foolery" as he called it, but in matters of horsemanship the rules were strict and his word was law. Any infraction such as bringing a horse home winded and sweating, and his blue eyes could turn awfully cold, and you'd better have a good excuse. He had learned in a harsh school that survival could depend on not making a mistake, particularly in regard to the horse you were riding. If anything happened to it you were afoot and helpless. We were taught to ride safely and well, to ensure our welfare and the horse's. Riding was more than just sticking on and going fast. It was learning about the vulnerable parts of a horse: withers, back, stifle joint, mouth, and hooves, and how to prevent colic, founder, cinch gall, rope burn, and wire cuts.

Mother had two good little verses about horsemanship:

> Your head and your heart keep bravely up,
>
> Your heels and your hands keep down,
>
> Your knees keep close to the horse's side
>
> And your elbows close to your own.

And,

> Up hill hurry me not,
>
> Downhill worry me not,
>
> On the level let me trot
>
> But do not water me when I'm hot.

There could never be anything slipshod about our gear and the way it was put on the horse. Bridles, saddles, and blankets had to be correct and carefully checked. When we were small we had to have tapidoros (taps) on our stirrups so our feet couldn't slip through. Getting hung up or dragged is a cowboy's nightmare. Likewise we were taught the proper knots to use when we tied up a horse – a slip knot was a dirty word – and how not to get into trouble with a lariat. Even the right way to tie your coat on behind, so it would not come loose and scare the horse. Another of his wise teachings was how to read the weather, the way the wind acts when there's going to be a change, and the look of the clouds before a hail storm. In spite of all his precautions we had wrecks; saddles turned, coats were lost, we got caught in storms, and sometimes we bit the dirt. The toughest lesson of all was when you go off you get up and climb on again.

We lived in close proximity with our beloved horses. They kept the grass mowed in the house yard. Dad's Pilot had been taught to shake hands and often ripped the window screens with his great hoof in his effort to greet us. Mary and I spent hours in the rickety little stable, currying the horses, polishing hooves, braiding their manes and tails, sometimes making wild flower wreaths to go around their necks. They were probably better groomed than we were. On hot days we lugged pails of water up the ladder to the loft and gave them shower baths through the wide spaces between the floorboards. Once Mary tried to give the Shetland an enema with a wine bottle. Her vocation for nursing was always strong.

Next to the stable was the feed and tack room and attached to it was the chicken house where a few gallant hens battled it out with all manner of predators. Skunks, weasels, badgers, or coyotes were always tunneling under the hen house. Loud squawks and Dad would run for the 22. The root cellar was dug into the bank, a dark spooky cave with cobwebs and a musty smell. The inner chamber held vegetables, and in the outer one Mother kept her preserves and bottles of wine and the perishable food in a screened cupboard.

Dad put up a sturdy swing beside the house, which everyone enjoyed. Mary and I liked to twist the rope tighter and tighter and then unwind with a horrible seasick sensation, but Mother had a more daring stunt. She could "skin the cat," pumping herself higher and higher and sailing over the top. It was scary to watch. Dad's special preserve was the woodpile where he did his morning calisthenics using the axe for an Indian club, swinging it around his head in great arcs. He was a mighty man with an axe and could make the chips fly. There was always a pile of willow fence posts to be sharpened. The kids' job was to hold the post upright while he swung the axe. It was almost as awful as when he wielded the post maul. The woodshed had a flat roof piled high with Dad's useful "junk" rolls of wire, rake teeth, and mower parts. Mary and I used it for our office and bolt hole when company came.

The pumps and the well near the back door supplied our water. One of Dad's quirks was his passion for a cold drink of water. It was his idea of a great treat, the nicest social gesture to a visitor, and a cure-all for everything from headache to cheering up a child. A milk cow brought up from Midway for the summer lived "the life of Riley" in the hayfield. The only demands made on her were that she stay away from stinkweed, and show up at milking time. Mother had learned to milk as Dad was so often away. She usually had a good relationship with Bossy, who would stand to be milked wherever Mother found her, but sometimes she drew one whose idea of fun was a game of hide and seek in the brush.

One of the first jobs in the spring when we came up from Midway was ploughing our little garden patch. Dad believed in making the most of kid power and devised a system where light shafts on the walking plough were attached to the saddle horses' necks by a collar. Mary could ride and steer, while Dad guided the plough. We grew vegetables to last the summer, and masses of flowers. We liked to visit the garden before breakfast, to see what had come out overnight. It smelled so lovely in the early morning. Dad's favourites were the big red poppies.

Beside the garden was "the Grove" a pretty little stand of willow, which was used for an outdoor living room. We often had our meals here. Mother and Dad liked to eat outside, and thought it was worth the extra work of toting food back and forth. Mary and I used it for a playhouse, where we kept our stable of stick horses. We got quite skilful at making rooms by lacing branches in and out to form walls. When we got bored with the house plan we took it apart and started again. The hammock hung between two trees for afternoon siestas. Mother and Dad entertained visitors with picnics and corn roasts. Many of our Sunset photos have the grove as a background, groups of people sitting on rugs on the grass, and Mary and I had our birthday parties there. There were many visitors in the summer; friends and relatives from the east sometimes came to stay for several weeks. Dad's old cronies would drop in to see him. That was the only time liquor appeared. Dad kept a bottle on hand to treat his special friends. Apart from that it was homemade wine, and raspberry vinegar for the children.

The wild berries were lush and plentiful in those days and Mother would invite her friends to come and pick. The best patches within walking distance were saved for her friends who didn't ride. Mary and I got very bored picking berries except for saskatoons, which often grew on such high bushes that we could stand on our saddles and strip the berries off in handfuls. We always gorged ourselves with dire results. When we were scattered out in the brush picking raspberries we would call back and forth, "my bottom's covered" or "is your bottom covered?" meaning the pail. People who weren't used to us thought it rather funny. Poor Mother always wore her English riding boots, which had slippery soles. So often she would just get her pail filled, and she'd slip and fall. All that work for nothing! It wasn't easy carrying two pails of berries home on horseback. We usually sat in a handful of them and the saddles were stained purple. A lot of work went into a winter's supply of jam and preserves.

Even the drive from Nanton to the ranch was an adventure with those early cars that overheated on steep grades. The road was graded as far as William's Coulee. After that it was little more than a broad trail which angled off to the left past the old buffalo jump and up through the hills, with wire gates to open. It was impassable in wet weather. The trail past our house was used as a shortcut to the main road by local traffic. Some of those picturesque travellers were right out of the old west, buggies, buckboards and wagons, hard bitten cowboys, hunters with hounds and pack horses, all passed our door. A steep knoll hid our immediate view of the trail from the west, so people would be upon us before we knew it. This is

A.2 Constance Ings picking berries with her pony Daffy (c.1924). Courtesy of Loree family.

how the visiting Indians would descend on us. One day Mother was busy in the kitchen when she heard a sound at the back door. Thinking it was the dog she called out, "no use hanging around with a hungry look on your face. I'm not going to feed you!" An embarrassed cowboy meekly said "Please, Ma'am, I just wanted a word with Mr. Ings."

On warm nights we hauled our bedding to the top of the knoll and slept out. No foamies or sleeping bags in those days. We lay on ticks stuffed with timothy hay, and had lots of sweaters and blankets, for it got cold towards morning. Mother would tell stories, and show us the constellations, and tell us the names of the stars. It was perfect when Dad would come too, for we didn't worry as much about the coyotes that used to come awfully close.

The knoll made a dandy sliding hill when it snowed in the late fall. There was a little pond at the bottom, and we could scoot down the hill and right across it. It was on the knoll that we first saw skis used. A Norwegian family worked on the ranch, and the older boys made themselves skis, steaming the wood to curve the tips. They worked fine, too. Mother loved to snowshoe, having done so much in Ontario as a girl. On one side of the knoll Mary and I had our dolls' cemetery. She and I rode back there years later and we could still find the little headstones.

Sunset was an ideal ranch in many ways: good streams, open land for grazing, some cultivated land where we grew oats, and a sheltered hay flat a mile long between two ranges of hills where cattle could be wintered. A mile down the trail and over the hill from our house was "Headquarters" where the main work of the ranch was done. Here there was a good spring, a set of corrals with cattle-working facilities, a house for the stockman, a bunkhouse for the riders, a stable and outbuildings. The haying equipment, wagons, and implements were kept here. The cattle were driven up from Midway in the spring after calving. The cattle drive could take twelve hours, a long tiresome day's ride with no trucks or horse trailers to make it easier. Sometimes a wagon would go along to pick up the exhausted calves. Usually something funny or interesting would happen to break the monotony of the trip. A flock of bluebirds perched on the telephone wire like a blue ribbon might lift our spirits and a sudden squall of rain with a biting wind would certainly dampen them. A fond memory is of coming home in the evening after a ride, and being met with the marvellous smell of supper cooking – partridges roasting, baked beans and homemade bread, and always the fragrance of willow smoke.

The branding was done at Headquarters later in the summer. Dad roped well and heeling was his long suit. Just as we do it today, one or two ropers on horseback rope the calf by the hind feet and drag it over to the branding crews. The roper has to be fast and accurate so as not to keep the crews waiting. The cattle were pastured on all the hill land, the Lake, the Heare place, as well as Sunset, so we were always riding, looking for strays, cutting out beef, checking fences, moving cattle from one field to another. It was an honour for a kid to be allowed to go along, let alone take a minor part in the cattle work. Dad was kind about letting me ride behind his saddle on Pilot, if it was just a routine ride, and Mary had to put up with me bouncing along behind her, before I graduated to the Shetland. At first I had to have someone hold the lead line, until it was thought safe to let me solo. Daffy was a pretty, nice-gaited little pony but full of devilish tricks. He ran away with us, he rolled in rivers, he reared and bucked, and ran in and bit other horses' stomachs without missing a step. Mary and I loved him dearly, and rode him for years.

A.3 Matriarch Edith Ings, an avid horsewoman (c.1940). Courtesy of Loree family.

The sound accompaniment of those years is hoof beats. It was bliss to have all that beautiful country for our playground. We explored every corner of Sunset, giving our own names to significant spots. We each had a mountain: two little hills, side by side. Mary Ings Mountain was steeper, but Conna Ings Mountain was bigger, and it was a tradition that we rolled down them on Halloween. Mother had an effective way of keeping us away from known hazards. The caved-in well had a bad fairy in it, and the boggy slough was where a wicked witch lived, and you couldn't have paid us to go near them.

Dad's riding had slowed down to Pilot's fast running walk. He rode because he had to, and he couldn't take a full day in the saddle. For Mother there could never be enough riding. Even if she was tired after a day's housework, a ride would restore her like nothing else. Bad weather didn't deter her; she loved riding in the wind and rain and could stand cold better than anyone. She was the ringleader in our adventures, and sometimes we found her a bit daunting. Mary and I might be asleep in our beds and be jolted awake by Mother's "Girls! Girls! Get up! It's a perfect night for a ride." How did we ever find our horses, let alone see to saddle them – it wasn't always a full moon. Riding in the dark didn't bother us. The horses knew the way, and it was cool and invigorating after a hot day. The nocturnal adventures, like a porcupine crossing our path, or a cow jumping out of the bushes, or meeting another night traveller, gave us something to laugh about and remember.

Her horse was usually fast and frisky, and we had a time to keep up to her. She wasn't the type of mother who said "Now children, be careful." It was more like "here's a flat place. Let's gallop!" Many of our rides were from Sunset to Midway or Nanton. It took two hours each way. Some were planned ahead but often they were impromptu. We might be bored at Midway and decide it would be fun to go to Sunset, and often the impulse hit us at an inconvenient time. Mary and I carried some strange burdens on those rides. Once it was the bread dough, which wasn't quite ready for the oven, another time a kettle of citron marmalade carried between us on a broom handle. One late fall exodus from the ranch involved two very large cats, each stuffed in a flour sack, squalling and spitting. How the horses hated that! We decided that there was one advantage to riding a wild horse – you didn't have to carry as much. On one night ride down from the ranch, Mary fell asleep and fell off "kerplunk" in the road. Mother had a pet saying which applied to our doings, "it's great to be crazy!"

This was the pattern of our time at Sunset, going up in the spring for brief stays, then moving up permanently when the weather turned nice. I vaguely remember the excitement and upheaval of those moves, loading up the democrat with our worldly goods, and the parents arguing about what was going and what was staying, and some things forgotten and others falling out. Dad had to spend more time at Midway than Mother, who would only come down to look after the house and garden, returning gladly to the hills, where it was always greener and cooler. When she was expecting me to be born, she drove down in the buggy to see the doctor, knowing her time was close. He advised her to either stay down, or return to the ranch immediately, which she did. I was born at sunset that same day, before the doctor arrived. Each fall the moving process would be reversed and it was seldom without drama: securing the cat at the last minute, and transporting the homemade wine, created a bit of excitement. No

A.4 Mary Ings on Daffy (far left) and local children riding to Sunset School (no date). Courtesy of Loree family.

matter how carefully it was packed, you could count on a bottle blowing its cork before it reached Midway.

Mary went off to the grandparents in London for the school year, which made all of us sad. Some years Mother couldn't bear to have her leave when September came and we stayed on through the glorious fall until nearly Christmas, before real winter weather drove us out. So it happened that both Mary and I began our education at Sunset school, and attended from time to time over the years. Every child should have the experience of going to a one-room country school. It was the only part of my school days that I thoroughly enjoyed. Sunset school still stands on the hill beside the road going north and south, a landmark visible for miles, commanding a wonderful view of the mountains and foothills and the prairies to the east. From there, on a clear night, you could see the lights of seven towns, and the red glow from the Turner Valley oilfields in the northwest. It is a neglected derelict now, but was once the centre of the community. In our time it was smart and trim with white paint and shining windows. A low red stable stood behind for the school ponies, for everyone came on horseback. There would be rousing games in the schoolyard at noon and recess – French and English, and Ante-I-Over. The shouts and shrieks of laughter drowned out the teacher's school bell. Outside on one wall was a large grill over the furnace vent, which made a perfect sound conductor.

We lined up to listen to the teacher bawling out someone kept in at recess, or counting the blows if she was wielding the strap. It was too bad for us if we were caught eavesdropping.

The schoolroom was sunny and cheerful, and very typical of its time: the teacher's desk up at the front under the flag and the pictures of "Their Majesties" and the pull-down maps, a piano, a glass-fronted bookcase, a bench with water pail and dipper. The big black furnace had a jacket, which swung out against the wall to make the girls' dressing room, where we could change out of our riding clothes. Coats and mitts were hung over the jacket to dry on wet days, and the smell of wet clothes and scorched wool was pretty strong. Frozen lunch pails and bottles of ink were put on top to thaw out, and the ceiling was decorated with blue splatters. The long blackboard had a trimming of stencil design, changed with the seasons, done with coloured chalk. Sometimes one of the "big kids" were allowed to do this, and I remember watching with pride as Mary did the "Sunbonnet Sues" and thinking the family had never before had such an honour. There were rows of desks of various sizes to fit the pupils who also came in various sizes, ages six to sixteen, grades one to eight. It tested the mettle of a teacher to keep everyone working at their own level. It was rather like a very large family, everybody paying a great deal of attention to what everybody else was doing. We had no secrets from one another, and the poor teacher wasn't allowed to have many either. Everyone in the district was interested in her public and private life.

She usually struck the right note with these free and uninhibited children, enough discipline to keep order, without disparaging, or squelching high spirits. Apart from the usual teasing and pushing and shoving the children were kind to one another. The older ones looked out for the little ones and showed the natural courtesy which was a trait of hill people. All ages had fun together in spelling bees, sing songs, marching drills, practicing for the Christmas concert, and making Halloween decorations.

The Halloween parties were memorable – popcorn balls, bobbing for apples, spooky games, and costumes. I remember Mary and I going home at noon to get ready. She was a ghost, with eye holes cut in a white sheet, and Mother dressed me as a black cat, with a stuffed black silk stocking for a tail. The horse wanted no part of us, but Mother helped us get on, me riding behind Mary. The sheet flapped, and the cat's tail thumped the horse's rump and it bucked all the way up the hill to the school, with us laughing so hard we could hardly hang on.

It was at Sunset school that we had our first look at royalty. The teacher got word that the Prince of Wales would be driving past on his way to the EP Ranche. We lined up to watch him pass. He smiled and waved but didn't stop.

Everybody turned out when there was a dance at Sunset, local families, farmers from the flats, and cowboys from the back ranches. The schoolyard was crowded with buggies, buckboards, and wagons, and a line of saddle horses was tied to the fence. The school would be lit up like a Christmas tree. The desks were stowed in the shed, and long benches put along the walls, one side for males, one side for females. The floor was sprinkled with corn meal to make it slippery as glass. The men would hang around outside on the porch until the music started up, while the women were busy in the teacherage laying out the lunch they had brought: husky sandwiches, pickles, and cake. The coffee was made in a copper boiler on the teacher's stove. The ladies' coats were piled on her bed and the babies laid out on top. When the older children got sleepy, they were laid out on the benches or under them. Hill children learned to dance very young, since they had been coming to these affairs since babyhood. The floor manager was the master of ceremonies and called the square dances. Local musicians provided beautiful music. Sunset had some excellent fiddlers, and as well, there would be piano, accordion, banjo or guitar. The dance would begin sedately enough, spirits and music would heat up as the night went on, until the building seemed to jump up and down on its foundation with the stomping feet and the beat and throb of the music. At midnight the floor manager would call, "get your partner for the supper waltz." The lunch was set out on the teacher's desk and everyone would fall to. Usually at this point some local talent would be talked into singing a cowboy song or doing a step dance. Then, everyone having got their second wind, the dance would go on till daylight, when people could see to go home. Sunset School has seen some high old times.

The depression didn't come suddenly. Times had never been that good and they kept getting worse and worse. Finally, there was a buyer for Sunset and Dad sold it. It was the bitterest pill we ever had to swallow, and so ended that chapter of our lives. The little house burned down a few years later.

Thank goodness we still had the Heare place. We made the house habitable, after a series of tenants or squatters; moved in, and set about to discover and explore all over again. Up till then we weren't too familiar with the place except as a day to the Canyon, a favourite picnic spot. When we had learned the trails and discovered all the beauties of the ranch we came to love it very much. Sunset was gentle country. This was more rugged, higher hills and faster streams. Trail's End, as Mother named it, saved our sanity during the drought and dust storm years. The prairies were very depressing: black walls of dust that blotted out the sun, howling, pitiless winds blowing our fields away. The trees were smothered, Mother's flowerbed killed out. The house was often so filled with dust, that you couldn't discern the pattern of the wallpaper. You would wake up in the morning to find your blanket was black with it. Nothing would keep it out. Childlike, I thought it was great fun to play in the sand dunes and ride my pony over the stone wall on the drifts. Mother battled that dust for all she was worth, but she couldn't win. There was always more. The least little wind would bring it sifting in again.

She fought a gallant battle against the depression too, cutting up her dresses and remaking clothes for me to wear to school, concocting good meals out of very little. Some of her hard time recipes became family favourites for years to come. Her egg-less, butter-less, milk-less cake was simply delicious. We didn't mind being poor, we had always lived frugally, but the terrible anxiety and the shame of being in debt, plus being short of feed for the cattle, and them not worth anything, was very, very hard. What brought the depression home to me was seeing Mother in a cheap, hideous brown dress that she had ordered from the catalogue. It just looked awful, scratchy and shapeless and ugly. That hurt me so much. Writing Dad's memoirs was good therapy for them both, and the articles were well received.

When Dad died in 1936, and then her parents too, Mother didn't lose any time in putting her life together again. She had a ranch to run, and a burden of debt to pay off. She started off by sprucing up the house, as best she could, with fresh paints and new curtains, which better expressed her personality. The house in the hills was re-designed with many improvements done at minimal cost, but very effective, and Trail's End was opened as a dude ranch. It started out on a very small scale, but the word spread through advertising, and satisfied customers who came back year after

A.5 Edith Ings at the Canyon, the favourite picnic spot on Trail's End Ranch (c.1950). Courtesy of Loree family.

year, and soon she was very well filled. During the war, airmen stationed at Vulcan and Claresholm and High River loved to come for their forty-eight hour leaves. It was her war effort, to give these boys a wonderful weekend.

Sometimes she was a one-man band. She would meet the buses, cook the meals and wash dishes, make beds, tend the vegetable garden, pick berries for pies and cobblers, saddle the horses, take the dudes riding, and still have enough energy at night to dress up like a lady and play cards with them and tell them stories. When finally the debts were paid off, instead of resting on her laurels, she borrowed money to buy two adjoining pieces of hill land to bring the ranch up to what it had been before Sunset was sold. Mother, you were a brave woman. I salute you.

Notes

Introduction

1 Violet LaGrandeur, "Memoirs of a Cowboy's Wife," 14, 72–27/SE, Provincial Archives of Alberta, Edmonton.

2 Ibid.

3 An extensive historiography of farm women exists, including several Canadian examples: Linda Rasmussen et al., eds., *A Harvest Yet to Reap: A History of Prairie Women* (Toronto: The Women's Press, 1976); Veronica Strong-Boag, "Pulling in Double Harness or Hauling a Double Load: Women, Work and Feminism on the Canadian Prairie," in *The Prairie West: Historical Readings*, 2nd ed., ed. R. Douglas Francis and Howard Palmer (Edmonton: University of Alberta Press, 1992), 401–23; Mary Kinnear, "'Do You Want Your Daughter to Marry a Farmer?': Women's Work on the Farm, 1922," in *Canadian Papers in Rural History*, vol. 6, ed. Donald H. Akenson (Gananoque, ON: Langdale, 1988),137–53.

4 Alice Marriott, *Hell on Horses and Women* (Norman: University of Oklahoma Press, 1953). This popular phrase usually finishes off ". . . and heaven for men and dogs."

5 A leather cover over the front of the stirrup, originating from the Spanish *vaquero* tradition and used for protection from brush, cattle, and weather. On children's saddles, *tapaderos* (or "taps") are used as a safety precaution, so that a small foot cannot slip through the stirrup.

6 Susan H. Armitage and Elizabeth Jameson, eds., *The Women's West* (Norman: University of Oklahoma, 1987).

7 Elizabeth Jameson, "Connecting the Women's Wests," in *One Step over the Line: Toward a History of Women in the North American Wests*, ed. Elizabeth Jameson and Sheila McManus (Edmonton: University of Alberta Press, 2008), 16. This is the authoritative text on the formative stages of western women's history.

8 See, for example, Peggy Pascoe, "Western Women at the Cultural Crossroads," in *Trails: Toward a New Western History*, ed. Patricia Nelson Limerick, Clyde A. Milner, and Charles E. Rankin (Lawrence: University Press of Kansas, 1991), 40–58.

9 R. W. Slatta, *Comparing Cowboys and Frontiers* (Norman: University of Oklahoma Press, 1997), 193–94.

10 Pascoe, "Cultural Crossroads," 44.

11 This usage of gender was first proposed by Joan Scott, in "Gender: A Useful Category of Historical Analysis," *American Historical Review* 91, no. 5 (1986): 1053–75.

12 Sarah Carter, "'He Country in Pants' No Longer: Diversifying Ranching History," in *Cowboys, Ranchers and the Cattle Business: Cross Border Perspectives on Ranching History*, ed. Sarah Carter, Simon Evans and Bill Yeo (Calgary: University of Calgary Press, 1997), 155; Sheilagh S. Jameson, "Women in the Southern Alberta Ranch Community, 1881–1914," in *The Canadian West: Social Change and Economic Development*, ed. Henry C. Klassen (Calgary: University of Calgary, Comprint Publishing, 1977), 63–78; Lewis G. Thomas, *Ranchers' Legacy: Alberta Essays*, ed. Patrick E. Dunae (Edmonton: University of Alberta Press, 1986).

13 Carter, "Diversifying Ranching History," 156, 160.

14 *Census of Prairie Provinces, 1916: Population and Agriculture* (Ottawa: 1918).

15 Warren M. Elofson, *Cowboys, Gentlemen, and Cattle Thieves: Ranching on the Western Frontier* (Montreal and Kingston: McGill-Queen's University Press, 2000), 20–21.

16 For an extensive collection of modern ranching women's life stories, see Thelma Poirier et al., eds., *A Voice of Her Own* (Calgary: University of Calgary Press, 2005).

17 Thomas, *Ranchers' Legacy*. Another argument for entrenched Old World culture on the frontier is found in Patrick Dunae, *Gentlemen Emigrants: From the British Public Schools to the Canadian Frontier* (Vancouver: Douglas & McIntyre, 1981).

18 David H. Breen, *The Canadian Prairie West and the Ranching Frontier, 1874–1924* (Toronto: University of Toronto Press, 1983). On the culture of the big ranches, see also Edward Brado, *Cattle Kingdom: Early Ranching in Alberta* (Surrey, BC: Heritage House, 2004).

19 Terry C. Jordan, *North American Cattle-Ranching Frontiers: Origins, Diffusion, Differentiation* (Albuquerque: University of New Mexico Press, 1993). For a similar argument, see Slatta, *Comparing Cowboys and Frontiers*.

20 Elofson, *Cowboys, Gentlemen, and Cattle Thieves*; Elofson, *Frontier Cattle Ranching in the Land and Times of Charlie Russell* (Montreal and Kingston: McGill-Queen's University Press, 2004).

21 Linda Hussa, *The Family Ranch: Land, Children, and Tradition in the American West* (Reno: University of Nevada Press, 2009), ix.

22 Elliott West, *Growing Up with the Country: Childhood on the Far Western Frontier* (Albuquerque: University of New Mexico Press, 1989), 74.

23 Jameson, "Connecting the Women's Wests," 19.

24 Elizabeth Lane, "A Brief Sketch of Memories of My Family," M652, George and Elizabeth Lane fonds, Glenbow Archives, Calgary (hereafter, Lane fonds).

25 Thomas, *Ranchers' Legacy*, 14.

26 Moira O'Neil [Agnes Skrine], "A Lady's Life on a Ranche," in *Blackwoods* (1898), reprinted in High River Pioneers' and Old Timers' Association (hereafter, High River), *Leaves from the Medicine Tree: A History of the Area Influenced by the Tree, and Biographies of Pioneers and Old Timers Who Came Under Its Spell prior to 1900* (Altona, MB: Friesen, 1960), 502.

27 Carter, "Diversifying Ranching History," 156–57.

28 Sheila McManus, "Mapping the Alberta-Montana Borderlands: Race, Ethnicity and Gender in the Late Nineteenth Century," *Journal of American Ethnic History* 20, no. 3 (2001): 71–88.

29 Ann Stoler quoted in Ibid., 72; McManus, "Mapping the Borderlands," 73.

30 Mary Daley. "A Letter from Mary." In *Cowgirls: 100 Years of Writing the Range*, ed. Thelma Poirier (Red Deer, AB: Red Deer College Press, 1997), 87–88

31 LaGrandeur, "Memoirs of a Cowboy's Wife."

32 Fred Ings to Edith Scatcherd, 8 November 1910, Loree family.

33 Carol Fairbanks and Sara Brooks Sundberg, "Farm Women on the Canadian Prairie Frontier: The Helpmate Image," in *Farm Women on the Prairie Frontier: A Sourcebook for Canada and the United States* (Metuchen: Scarecrow, 1983), 79.

34 Jacqueline Chalmers, interview by Rachel Herbert, 31 March 2011, Nanton, AB.

35 Mary Nichols, letter (recipient unknown), 10 December 1909, property of Jacqueline Chalmers, Claresholm, AB.

36 Ibid.

37 Chalmers, interview.

38 Thomas, *Ranchers' Legacy*, 10.

39 Mary Kinnear, *A Female Economy: Women's Work in a Prairie Province, 1870–1970* (Montreal and Kingston: McGill-Queen's University Press, 1998), 95.

40 "Mary Guenther," in Poirier et al., *A Voice of Her Own*, 211–12.

Chapter 1

1 Dee Garceau, "Single Women Homesteaders and the Meanings of Independence: Places on the Map, Places in the Mind," *Frontiers: A Journal of Women Studies* 15, no. 3 (1995): 3.

2 Ibid.

3 L. V. Kelly, *The Range Men: The Story of the Ranchers and Indians of Alberta* (1913; Toronto: Coles, 1980).

4 Breen, *The Canadian Prairie West*, 19.

5 Kelly, *The Range Men*, 113.

6 Ibid., 156.

7 Agnes Morley Cleaveland, *No Life for a Lady* (Boston: Houghton Mifflin, 1941), 37.

8 Breen, *The Canadian Prairie West*, 25.

9 Catherine A. Cavanaugh, "No Place for a Woman: Engendering Western Canadian Settlement," *Western Historical Quarterly* 28, no. 4 (1997): 494.

10 Frederick Jackson Turner, "The Significance of the Frontier in American History," in *Major Problems in the History of the American West: Documents and Essays*, ed. Clyde A. Milner (Lexington, MA: Heath, 1989), 2–21.

11 Walter P. Webb, *The Great Plains* (New York: Ginn & Company, 1931), 207; my emphasis.

12 Cavanaugh, "No Place for a Woman," 495.

13 Henry C. Klassen, *Eye on the Future: Business People in Calgary and the Bow Valley, 1870–1900* (Calgary: University of Calgary Press, 2002), 307.

14 Ibid., 308.

15 Ibid.; "The Bedingfelds," in High River, *Leaves from the Medicine Tree*, 72.

16 "The Prince's Purchase," *High River Times*, 23 October 1919.

17 Clifford Sifton quoted in Cavanaugh, "No Place for a Woman," 504.

18 Catherine Cavanaugh, "The Limitations of the Pioneering Partnership: The Alberta Campaign for Homestead Dower, 1909–1925," *Canadian Historical Review* 74, no. 2 (1993): 199.

19 Ibid.

20 Mrs. George Cran, *A Woman in Canada* (Toronto: Musson Book Company, 1910), 153.

21 Ibid., 154. The term "proving up" refers to making the required improvements on the land in order for legal ownership to be granted to the homesteader— the basic stipulations being an established primary residence and specific acreage of land put into agricultural use .

22 Glenda Riley, *Women and Nature: Saving the "Wild" West* (Lincoln: University of Nebraska Press, 1999), 11.

23 Elinore Pruitt Stewart, *Letters of a Woman Homesteader* (1914; Boston: Houghton Mifflin, 1988), 215.

24 Wilfrid Eggleston, *Homestead on the Range* (Ottawa: Borealis, 1982), 8.

25 Ibid.

26 "Murphy Family," in Pincher Creek Historical Society (hereafter, Pincher Creek), *"Prairie Grass to Mountain Pass": History of the Pioneers of Pincher Creek and District* (Calgary: Friesen, 1974), 131.

27 Nanton and District Historical Society (hereafter, Nanton), *Mosquito Creek Roundup: Nanton-Parkland* (Calgary: Friesen, 1975), 57.

28 Georgina H. Thomson, *Crocus and Meadowlark Country: A Story of an Alberta Family* (Edmonton: Institute of Applied Art, 1963), 150.

29 "On Pine Creek," *Calgary Tribune*, 8 July 1887.

30 Ibid.

31 Ibid.

32 "Women Ranchers," *Calgary Herald*, 21 October 1902.

33 Ibid.

34 Ibid.

35 Cavanaugh, "Limitations of the Pioneering Partnership," 204.

36 For a thorough explication of the fight for dower rights, see Cavanaugh, "Limitations of the Pioneering Partnership."

37 "District Brands," in Nanton, *Mosquito Creek Roundup*, 81–86.

38 Stavely Historical Book Society (hereafter, Stavely), *The Butte Stands Guard: Stavely and District* (Calgary: Friesen, 1976), 21–24.

39 Elofson, *Frontier Cattle Ranching*, 20–21.

40 Evelyn C. Springett, *For My Children's Children* (Montreal: Unity Press, 1937), 120.

41 Monica Hopkins, *Letters from a Lady Rancher* (Halifax: Formac, 1983), 61.

42 Maxine Macleay and Dorothy Macleay, *The Rocking P Gazette*, November 1923, property of Clay Chattaway, Nanton, AB.

43 Maxine Macleay and Dorothy Macleay, *The Rocking P Gazette*, December 1923, property of Clay Chattaway, Nanton, AB.

44 Springett, *For My Children's Children*, 121–22.

45 Ibid.

46 Ibid.

47 Rhoda Sivell, "The Motherless Calf," in *Voices from the Range* (Toronto: T. Eaton Co., 1911), 30.

48 Ann Clifford, *Ann's Story: A Great Ranching Empire and the People Who Made It Work* (N.p.: Forever in Memory, 1995).

49 *Rocking P Gazette*, February 1925.

Chapter 2

1 Warren M. Elofson, *Somebody Else's Money: The Walrond Ranch Story, 1883–1907* (Calgary: University of Calgary Press, 2009), 15. This book contains a thorough explication of the failings of one of the largest open-range ranches.

2 Elofson, *Frontier Cattle Ranching*, 37.

3 Barry Potyondi, *In Palliser's Triangle: Living in the Grasslands, 1850–1930* (Saskatoon: Purich, 1995), 57.

4 Klassen, *Eye on the Future*, 171.

5 Breen, *The Canadian Prairie West*, 166.

6 Elofson, *Cowboys, Gentlemen, and Cattle Thieves*, 20.

7 Klassen, *Eye on the Future*, 317.

8 Breen, *The Canadian Prairie West*, 64–65; Henry C. Klassen, "A Century of Ranching at the Rocking P and Bar S," in *Cowboys, Ranchers and the Cattle Business: Cross Border Perspectives on Ranching History*, ed. Sarah Carter, Simon Evans, and Bill Yeo (Calgary: University of Calgary Press, 1997), 101–22.

9 Elofson, *Cowboys, Gentlemen, and Cattle Thieves*, 19.

10 For an exhaustive look at patterns of land use and the complexities of lease regulations in the industry from 1881 to 1948, see Max Foran, *Trails and Trials: Markets and Land Use in Alberta Beef Cattle Industry, 1881–1948* (Calgary: University of Calgary Press, 2003).

11 Brado, *Cattle Kingdom*, 194.

12 This thesis runs throughout Elofson's work. For his explanation of evolving ranching methods, see Elofson, *Frontier Cattle Ranching*, chap. 6.

13 Kelly, *The Range Men*, 52.

14 Breen, *The Canadian Prairie West*, 167.

15 M2487, Robert Newbolt fonds, Glenbow Archives, Calgary (hereafter, Newbolt fonds). In a study of land use in the early cattle industry, Max Foran notes that although barley was a productive feed crop among ranchers, it was "not the 'done thing' to sow much barley" prior to the 1920s. Foran, *Trails and Trials*, 224.

16 Ibid.

17 The A7 Ranche at Nanton, Alberta, is an example of a carefully managed ranch that uses year-round grazing. Few ranches in Alberta have the land base, or the skilled management, to graze cattle year-round. However, as grass management evolves, more ranches are beginning to utilize stockpiled grass for winter grazing. See http://www.a7ranche.com.

18 *Census of Prairie Provinces, 1916: Population and Agriculture* (Ottawa: 1918), 49, table 32.

19 Elofson, *Frontier Cattle Ranching*, 163.

20 Mary Neth, *Preserving the Family Farm: Women, Community, and the Foundations of Agribusiness in the Midwest, 1900–1940* (Baltimore: Johns Hopkins University Press, 1995), 26.

21 Elofson, *Somebody Else's Money*, 17.

22 Isabel F. Randall, *A Lady's Ranch Life in Montana*, ed. Richard L. Saunders (Norman: University of Oklahoma Press, 2004), 91.

23 Catherine B. Dick, "The Bond Family of Tongue Creek," in Tales and Trials History Book Society (hereafter, Tales and Trials), *Tales and Trials: A History of Longview and Surrounding Area* (Calgary: Northwest Printing and Lithography, 1977), 46.

24 "Dick Family," in Nanton, *Mosquito Creek Roundup*, 99–100.

25 "Austin Family," in Pincher Creek, *Prairie Grass to Mountain Pass*, 4–7.

26 "Lane Family," in Pincher Creek, *Prairie Grass to Mountain Pass*, 90.

27 *Rocking P Gazette*, March 1924.

28 "Pedersen Family," in Pincher Creek, *Prairie Grass to Mountain Pass*, 797.

29 Neth, *Preserving the Family Farm*, 32.

30 "Bateman Family," in Foothills Historical Society (hereafter, Foothills), *Chaps and Chinooks: A History West of Calgary* (Calgary: Foothills Historical Society, 1976), 257.

31 "John and Susan Copithorne Family," in Foothills, *Chaps and Chinook*, 261.

32 Ibid., 261–62.

33 "Porter Family," in Pincher Creek, *Prairie Grass to Mountain Pass*, 338.

34 Macleay and Macleay, *Rocking P Gazette*, March 1924. Sending one of the cowboys to town for the "grub stake" is noted as a monthly event.

35 For an example of a shopping list used to stock the Bar U Ranch store house, see Clifford, *Ann's Story*.

36 "May Family," in Foothills, *Chaps and Chinooks*, 273.

37 Maxine Macleay and Dorothy Macleay, *Rocking P Gazette*, January 1925, property of Clay Chattaway, Nanton, AB.

38 Evelyn Cochrane to Arthur Cochrane, 29 November 1900, Billy and Evelyn Cochrane Fonds, M6552-2, Glenbow Archive, Calgary (hereafter, Glenbow).

39 "Halton Family," in Pincher Creek, *Prairie Grass to Mountain Pass*, 52.

40 Ibid.

41 Hopkins, *Letters from a Lady Rancher*, 37.

42 Ibid.

43 Evelyn's diary, Billy and Evelyn Cochrane fonds, M6552-1, Glenbow.

44 Ibid.

45 Neth, *Preserving the Family Farm*, 18–19.

46 Hopkins, *Letters from a Lady Rancher*, 52.

47 Ibid.

48 Ibid.

49 Ibid.

50 Strong-Boag, "Pulling in Double Harness," 401–23.

51 O'Neil, "A Lady's Life on a Ranche," 508.

52 Garceau, "Single Women Homesteaders," 6.

53 Ibid., 12.

54 Randall, *A Lady's Ranch Life*, 117–18.

55 Completed in 1908, the house at the Midway Ranch was one of four homes built of sandstone from a quarry in the Nanton area. Only two, including the Midway, remain today. Lane, "A Brief Sketch."

56 Susan Margaret McKinnon St. Maur, *Impressions of a Tenderfoot* (London: John Murray, 1890), 47.

57 Randall, *A Lady's Ranch Life*, 62.

58 Thomas, *Ranchers' Legacy*, 14.

59 Ibid., 15–16.

60 "Rowe Family," in Pincher Creek, *Prairie Grass to Mountain Pass*, 552.

61 George Zarn, *Above the Forks* (High River, AB: published by author, 1978).

62 Robert Raynor, "The Feminine Cowboy," *Rocking P Gazette*, October 1924.

63 Maxine Macleay and Dorothy Macleay, *The Rocking P Gazette*, January 1924, property of Clay Chattaway, Nanton, AB.

64 Maxine Macleay and Dorothy Macleay, *The Rocking P Gazette*, September 1924, property of Clay Chattaway, Nanton, AB.

65 Maxine Macleay and Dorothy Macleay, *The Rocking P Gazette*, February 1924, property of Clay Chattaway, Nanton, AB.

66 Macleay and Macleay, *Rocking P Gazette*, January 1924.

67 All editions of the *Rocking P Gazette* list Dorothy and Maxine Macleay's activities; many are riding related, but a number of adventures also took place in the barnyard.

68 Klassen, "A Century of Ranching," 112, 113.

69 See chapter 6, "The Significance of Horses to Women's Emancipation," for a closer examination of women's work on horseback during the 1880s and 1890s.

70 After the turn of the century, virtually any family history contained in a local history book from a ranch district suggests that women did mounted cattle work. See, for example, "Mrs. Margery Lunn," in Pincher Creek, *Prairie Grass to Mountain Pass*, 103–4.

71 The term "feminine cowboys" appears in the October 1924 issue of the *Rocking P Gazette*.

72 Doris A. Burton, *Babe's Sunshine: I Made My Own* (Lethbridge: Robins Southern Printing, 1990), 52.

73 "Pioneer Days," 39, M4116, Mrs. Catherine Neil fonds, Glenbow (hereafter, Neil fonds).

74 Ibid., 46.

75 Nellie Hutchison-Taylor quoted in Foothills, *Chaps and Chinooks*, 239.

76 Ibid., 238.

77 Ibid., 239.

78 Ibid.

79 Ibid., 241.

80 Ibid.

81 Simon Evans, *Prince Charming Goes West: The Story of the E.P. Ranch* (Calgary: University of Calgary Press, 1993), 53.

82 "Gardner Family," in Nanton, *Mosquito Creek Roundup*, 57.

83 Zarn, *Above the Forks*. Zarn is comparing the typical family ranch to the A7 Ranche, backed by the legacy and funds of its founder, A. E. Cross, and his Calgary Brewing and Malting Company.

84 Elsie Lane Gordon quoted in Stavely, *The Butte Stands Guard*, 233.

85 Ibid.; Jennifer Barr, interview by Rachel Herbert, 25 March 2010, Oxley Ranch, AB.

86 Gordon quoted in *The Butte Stands Guard*, 233.

87 Demonstrating admirable foresight, and as a testament to the enduring legacy of her family, Jennifer Barr has preserved the Oxley ranch in perpetuity with the Nature Conservancy of Canada. Shawn Logan, "Nature Conservancy of Canada Acquires Historic 1882 Ranch near Stavely," *Calgary Herald*, March 29, 2017, http://calgaryherald.com/news/local-news/nature-conservancy-of-canada-acquires-historic-1882-ranch-near-stavely.

88 Ings family documents, Loree family. For an examination of the egalitarian nature of dude ranches and the freedom and adventure they offered women, see Riley, *Women and Nature*.

89 Kelly, *The Range Men*, 12.

90 Evelyn Cameron, "The 'Cowgirl' in Montana," in Poirier, *Cowgirls*, 65; St. Maur, *Impressions of a Tenderfoot*, 46.

Chapter 3

1 Thomas, *Ranchers' Legacy*, 15.

2 Linda Loree, interview by Rachel Herbert, 19 March 2010, Nanton, AB.

3 Elizabeth Maret, *Women of the Range: Women's Roles in the Texas Beef Cattle Industry* (College Station: Texas A&M University Press, 1993), 21.

4 Jeanne Kay, "Landscapes of Women and Men: Rethinking the Regional Historical Geography of United States and Canada," *Journal of Historical Geography* 17, no. 4 (1991): 443.

5 Ibid.

6 Ibid.

7 Maret, *Women of the Range*, 14–15.

8 Mary Ella Inderwick, "A Lady and Her Ranch," in *The Best from Alberta History*, ed. Hugh Dempsey (Saskatoon: Western Producer Prairie Books, 1981), 76.

9 Ibid., 74.

10 Ibid., 74–75.

11 Randall, *A Lady's Ranch Life*, 82.

12 Ibid., 83.

13 "Lou Forsaith," in Poirier et al., *A Voice of Her Own*, 255.

14 Hopkins, *Letters from a Lady Rancher*, 25.

15 Aritha van Herk, "Washtub Westerns," in *Unsettled Pasts: Reconceiving the West through Women's History*, ed. Sarah Carter et al. (Calgary: University of Calgary Press, 2005), 260.

16 Hopkins, *Letters from a Lady Rancher*, 14, 17.

17 Kay, "Landscapes of Women and Men," 445.

18 Neth, *Preserving the Family Farm*, 32.

19 Strong-Boag, "Pulling in Double Harness," 401–23.

20 Kinnear, "Women's Work on the Farm," 137–53.

21 Garceau, "Single Women Homesteaders," 16.

22 West, *Growing Up with the Country*, 139.

23 Susan Newcomb quoted in ibid., 140.

24 "Carley Cooper," in Poirer et al., *A Voice of Her Own*, 283.

25 Cavanaugh, "Limitations of the Pioneering Partnership," 207.

26 Burton, *Babe's Sunshine*, 55.

27 Cavanaugh, "Limitations of the Pioneering Partnership," 221.

28 Ibid., 52.

29 Ibid.

30 Hazel Cerney and Ethel Hunter, *The Silent Hills: The Kropinak Family of Chapel Rock* (Blairmore: Hazel Cerney, 1992), 13.

31 Ibid.

32 Rhoda Sivell, interview by Mae Laidlaw, Historical Society of Medicine Hat and District Fonds, Esplanade Archives, accessed 5 March 2010, http://archives.esplanade.ca.

33 Ibid.

34 Sivell, *Voices from the Range*, 46–47.

35 Neth, *Preserving the Family Farm*, 33.

36 Elliott West, "Families in the West," *OAH Magazine of History* 9, no. 1 (1994), 19.

37 "Joan Lawrence," in Poirier et al., *Voice of Her Own*, 160.

38 "Doris Fenton," in Poirier et al., *Voice of Her Own*, 433.

39 Vivian Bruneau Ellis quoted in Sherm Ewing, *The Range* (Missoula: Mountain Press Publishing, 1990), 65.

40 White, interview.

41 Lane, "A Brief Sketch," 22.

42 Ibid.

43 Ibid.

44 "Lenore Maclean," in Poirier, *Cowgirls*, 236.

45 See account ledger in Ings family documents, Loree family.

46 Brado, *Cattle Kingdom*, 80.

47 Springett, *For My Children's Children*; Elsie Lane Gordon quoted in Stavely, *The Butte Stands Guard*; White, interview.

48 West, "Families in the West," 19.

49 Cynthia Culver Prescott, "'Why She Didn't Marry Him': Love, Power, and Marital Choice on the Far Western Frontier," *Western Historical Quarterly* 38, no. 1 (2007): 26.

50 Barbara Handy-Marchello, *Women of the Northern Plains: Gender and Settlement on the Frontier Homestead, 1870–1930* (St. Paul: Minnesota Historical Society Press, 2005), 50.

51 Prescott, "Love, Power, and Marital Choice," 26.

52 West, *Growing Up with the Country*, 251.

53 James Fergus cited in Robert M. Horne, "James Fergus: Frontier Businessman, Miner, Rancher, Free Thinker" (PhD diss., University of Montana, 1971), chap. 4.

54 Ibid.

55 Nancy Young, "The Reins in Their Hands: Ranchwomen and the Horse in Southern Alberta 1880–1914," *Alberta History* 52, no. 1 (2004): 4.

56 "Bob Newbolt, Pioneer 1884, as told to Angus McKinnon," Newbolt fonds.

57 Ibid.

58 Cleaveland, *No Life for a Lady*, 145.

59 Macleay and Macleay, *Rocking P Gazette*, January 1924.

60 Maxine Macleay and Dorothy Macleay, *The Rocking P Gazette*, September 1923, property of Clay Chattaway, Nanton, AB.

61 "Richard and Sophia Copithorne Family," in Foothills, *Chaps and Chinooks*, 265.

62 "McCarthy Family," in Pincher Creek, *Prairie Grass to Mountain Pass*, 787.

63 Catherine Bond Dick, "You and I," in *Trails I've Ridden* (Calgary: Albertan Job Press, 1946), 26

64 Catherine Bond Dick, "Memories- 1931," in *Trails I've Ridden*, 26.

65 Fred Ings to Edith Scatcherd, 16 November 1910, Loree family.

66 Ibid.

67 Ibid.

68 West, *Growing Up with the Country*, 249.

Chapter 4

1 Local Alberta history books, such as *Chaps and Chinooks* by the Foothills Historical Society (Calgary, 1976), contain women's recollections of childbirth experiences. Also, a number of unusually forthright memoirs exist, such as those found in the Neil fonds, Glenbow.

2 Nanci Langford, "Childbirth on the Canadian Prairies, 1880–1930," in *Telling Tales: Essays in Western Women's History*, ed. Catherine A. Cavanaugh and Randi R. Warne (Vancouver: UBC Press, 2000), 148.

3 Ibid., 159, 171.

4 Nadine I. Kozak, "Advice Ideals and Rural Prairie Realities: National and Prairie Scientific Motherhood Advice, 1920–29," in *Unsettled Pasts: Reconceiving the West through Women's History*, ed. Sarah Carter et al. (Calgary: University of Calgary Press, 2005), 179–204.

5 "Edith Wearmouth," in Poirier et al., *A Voice of Her Own*, 14.

6 "Pioneer Days," 8, Neil fonds.

7 Langford, "Childbirth on the Canadian Prairies," 149.

8 Barbara Gardiner to Aunt Nellie, 23 November 1907, M7283-72, Glenbow.

9 Pioneer women speak candidly about reproductive issues and the veil of secrecy that surrounded them in Eliane Leslau Silverman, *The Last Best West: Women on the Alberta Frontier, 1880–1930* (Calgary: Fifth House, 1998) 79–95.

10 Hopkins, *Letters from a Lady Rancher*, 50.

11 "Doris Burton," in Poirier et al., *A Voice of Her Own*, 137.

12 Burton, *Babe's Sunshine*, 79.

13 West, *Growing Up with the Country*, 156.

14 Springett, *For My Children's Children*, 98.

15 LaGrandeur, "Memoirs of a Cowboy's Wife."

16 "Doris Fenton," in Poirier et al., *A Voice of Her Own*, 432.

17 Ibid.

18 "Pioneer Days," 27, Neil fonds.

19 Ibid., 58.

20 Ibid., 58–60.

21 Ibid., 26.

22 Ibid., 31.

23 "Augusta Hoffman," in Poirier, *Cowgirls*, 98.

24 Springett, *For My Children's Children*, 132.

25 Ibid., 98.

26 Ibid., 99.

27 Hopkins, *Letters from a Lady Rancher*, 50.

28 Ibid., 50.

29 Ibid., 51.

30 "Pioneer Days," 45, Neil fonds.

31 "E. J. Callaway Family," in Foothills, *Chaps and Chinooks*, 221.

32 Hopkins, *Letters from a Lady Rancher*, 50.

33 Langford, "Childbirth on the Canadian Prairies," 164.

34 Ings family documents, Loree family. For a similar example, see Nancy Millar, *The Unmentionable History of the West* (Calgary: Red Deer Press, 2006), 80. The four deaths in this case were attributed to "childbed fever brought on by the doctor who likely didn't wash his hands and equipment between deliveries."

35 May Ings to Fred Ings, 4 February 1898, Loree family.

36 Ibid.

37 Constance Loree, "My Sunset Childhood" (unpublished memoir, c.1970s), Loree family.

38 Neth, *Preserving the Family Farm*, 64.

39 "Manuscript of Memoirs," 3, M8193, Frank Lynch-Staunton fonds, box 2, file 23, Glenbow.

40 "James Young Family," in Foothills, *Chaps and Chinooks*, 223.

41 "McCarthy Family," in Pincher Creek, *Prairie Grass to Mountain Pass*, 784.

42 Ibid., 783–85.

43 "Pansy White-Brekhus," in Poirier et al., *A Voice of Her Own*, 196.

44 "Pioneer Days," 21, Neil fonds.

45 Kinnear, "Women's Work on the Farm," 138.

46 Philip Sheridan Long (as told by T. B. Long), *Seventy Years a Cowboy* (Saskatoon: Freeman, 1965), 38, 41.

Chapter 5

1 "Women Ranchers," *Calgary Herald*, 21 October 1902.

2 See photo of Edith Ings on the back cover of Fredrick W. Ings, *Before the Fences: Tales from the Midway Ranch* (Calgary: McAra, 1980).

3 *Okotoks Review*, 22 December 1911.

4 Springett, *For My Children's Children*, 120.

5 Ibid., 120.

6 "Kemmis Family," in Pincher Creek, *Prairie Grass to Mountain Pass*, 710.

7 Linda Loree, interview by Rachel Herbert, Nanton, AB, 19 March 2010.

8 Evelyn Cameron, "The 'Cowgirl' in Montana," 65–66.

9 Hopkins, *Letters from a Lady Rancher*, 18.

10 Ibid., 145.

11 Ibid., 145.

12 Ibid., 146.

13 Cameron, "Cowgirl," 66.

14 "Gage Family," in Stavely, *The Butte Stands Guard*, 227.

15 Cleaveland, *No Life for a Lady*, 242.

16 Teresa Jordan, *Cowgirls: Women of the American West*, 2nd ed. (Lincoln: University of Nebraska Press, 1992), 93.

17 Catherine B. Dick, "The Bond Family of Tongue Creek," in Tales and Trials, *Tales and Trials*, 46.

18 "Chappell Family," in Pincher Creek, *Prairie Grass to Mountain Pass*, 504.

19 "John Sexsmith and Family," in High River, *Leaves from the Medicine Tree*, 42.

20 White, interview.

21 Thomson, *Crocus and Meadowlark Country*, 179.

22 Thanks to Glenbow Museum senior curator Lorain Lounsberry for pointing out the significance of material artefacts and for a tour of the museum's saddles, crops, riding habits, and other related items (4 April 2007).

23 Cameron, "Cowgirl," 65

24 Ibid., 65.

25 Burton, *Babe's Sunshine*, 55.

26 See photograph of Anna Hanson (1905) in Elizabeth Clair Flood and William Manns, *Cowgirls: Women of the Wild West* (Santa Fe: Zon International, 2003).

27 Examples of these saddles are found in Lenore McLean's private tack collection in Longview, Alberta.

28 A brass horn saddle and a "mother and child saddle" were kept in our private tack collection in Nanton. The barn housing them burned down on February 13, 2015. Eleven saddles, including four family heirlooms, were lost. No animals were harmed in the fire.

29 R. T. Frazier Saddlery, catalogue no. 15 (Pueblo, CO, 1914), facsimile of original published by Old West Trading Company, 1995.

30 Maxine Macleay and Dorothy Macleay, *The Rocking P Gazette*, April 1925, property of Clay Chattaway, Nanton, AB.

31 Ibid.

32 See photograph in Jordan, *Cowgirls*, 211.

33 Tad Lucas quoted in Jordan, *Cowgirls*, 203. Rodeo women made the bulk of their own costumes, spending free time on the road designing and sewing and trying to make the garments fashionable and durable.

Chapter 6

1 Cleaveland, *No Life for a Lady*, 103.

2 For an examination of how ranching was pushed into more marginal and sparsely populated ecological zones, see Foran, *Trails and Trials*.

3 Ella Inderwick, letter of 13 May 1884, M559, Ella Inderwick fonds, Glenbow.

4 LaGrandeur, "Memoirs of a Cowboy's Wife."

5 Springett, *For My Children's Children*, 86.

6 Young, "Reins in Their Hands," 4.

7 Randall, *A Lady's Ranch Life*, 136.

8 Dorothy Blades, interview by Frank Jacobs for Stockmen's Memorial Foundation "Heritage Voices" project, c.1980s, Bert Sheppard Library and Archives, Cochrane, AB (hereafter, Sheppard Archives).

9 "Clark and Ethel Schlosser Family," in Stavely, *The Butte Stands Guard*, 367.

10 Ibid.

11 Cleaveland, *No Life for a Lady*, 65.

12 Elizabeth Lane, "Unpublished Reflections," 15, Lane fonds.

13 Ibid., 17.

14 "Carley Cooper," in Poirier et al., *A Voice of Her Own*, 284.

15 Edna Copithorne, interview by Jack Hawkwood for Stockmen's Memorial Foundation "Heritage Voices" project, c.1980s, Sheppard Archives.

16 Loree, "My Sunset Childhood."

17 "Louis Napolean Blache Family," in Foothills, *Chaps and Chinooks*, 214.

18 Loree, "My Sunset Childhood."

19 Ibid.

20 Evelyn Cochrane to Arthur Cochrane, 15 November 1900, M6552-2, Billy and Evelyn Cochrane fonds, Glenbow.

21 West, *Growing Up with the Country*, 88–89, 75.

22 Claude Gardiner, *Letters from an English Rancher*, ed. Hugh Dempsey (Calgary: Glenbow Alberta Institute, 1988), 53.

23 Ibid.

24 Nettie Smith, "Hillier Family," in Pincher Creek, *Prairie Grass to Mountain Pass*, 769.

25 "Gibson Family," in Foothills, *Chaps and Chinooks*, 271.

26 Cleaveland, *No Life for a Lady*, 127.

27 "Bessie Park MacEwan," in Foothills, *Chaps and Chinooks*, 313.

28 Augusta Hoffman, "Lost Child Creek," in Poirier, *Cowgirls*, 97.

29 Ibid.

30 Lorain Lounsberry, "Wild West Shows and the Canadian West," in *Cowboys, Ranchers and the Cattle Business: Cross Border Perspectives on Ranching History*, ed. Sarah Carter, Simon Evans, and Bill Yeo (Calgary: University of Calgary Press, 1997), 141.

31 "Lenore Maclean," in Poirier, *Cowgirls*, 234.

32 Jeanne Rhodes, "Fannie Sperry," in Poirier, *Cowgirls*, 237–38.

33 Jordan, *Cowgirls*, 191.

34 Hopkins, *Letters from a Lady Rancher*, 44.

35 Ibid., 4.

36 Ibid., 5.

37 Cleaveland, *No Life for a Lady*, 156.

38 Hopkins, *Letters from a Lady Rancher*, 17.

39 Inderwick, letter of 13 May 1884, Glenbow.

40 Springett, *For My Children's Children*, 170.

41 Blades, interview.

42 Evelyn Cochrane to Arthur Cochrane, 15 November 1900, M6552, Billy and Evelyn Cochrane fonds, Glenbow.

43 Ibid.

44 Gladys Baptie to Heritage park, 1972, M2551, Thomas and Gladys Baptie fonds, Glenbow.

45 "Hester Jane Robinson," in Foothills, *Chaps and Chinooks*, 284.

46 LaGrandeur, "Memoirs of a Cowboy's Wife," 5.

47 Lucy Seymour, interview by Orrin Hart for Stockmen's Memorial Foundation "Heritage Voices" project, c.1980s, Sheppard Archives.

48 Hopkins, *Letters from a Lady Rancher*, 135.

49 Catherine Bond Dick, "The Dick Ranch," in Nanton, *Mosquito Creek Roundup*, 100.

50 "Bob Newbolt, Pioneer 1884," Newbolt fonds.

51 Loree, "My Sunset Childhood."

52 Ibid.

53 "Trail's End Visitors Book and Log," summer 1931, Ings family documents, Loree family.

54 Hopkins, *Letters from a Lady Rancher*, 59.

55 Thomas, *Ranchers' Legacy*, 30.

56 "Louis Napolean Blache Family," in Foothills, *Chaps and Chinooks*, 46.

57 Ings, *Before the Fences*, 63.

58 Ibid, 60.

59 West, *Growing Up with the Country*, 106.

60 "Smith Family," in Pincher Creek, *Prairie Grass to Mountain Pass*, 343.

61 Randall, *A Lady's Ranch Life*, 121.

62 Hopkins, *Letters from a Lady Rancher*, 100–5.

63 Thomson, *Crocus and Meadowlark Country*, 157.

64 Loree, "My Sunset Childhood."

65 Inderwick, letter of 13 May 1884, Glenbow.

66 Loree, "My Sunset Childhood."

67 Inderwick, letter of 13 May 1884, Glenbow

68 Catherine Bond Dick, "The Dick Ranch," in Nanton, *Mosquito Creek Roundup*, 100.

69 Helen Clark, "A Horse beneath Me . . . Sometimes," in *Cowgirls*, 241.

70 Thomas, *Ranchers' Legacy*, 88.

Conclusion

1 Sarah Ellen Roberts quoted in Fairbanks and Sundberg, "Farm Women on the Canadian Prairie Frontier," 82.

2 Kay, "Landscapes of Women and Men," 448.

3 John W. Bennett, *Northern Plainsmen: Adaptive Strategy and Agrarian Life* (Chicago: Aldine, 1969), 179.

4 "Bob Newbolt, Pioneer 1884," Newbolt fonds.

5 O'Neil, "Lady's Life on a Ranche," 502, 503.

6 Ibid., 505.

7 Springett, *For My Children's Children*, 103.

8 Cleaveland, *No Life for a Lady*, 32

9 "Streeter Family," in Stavely, *The Butte Stands Guard*, 389.

10 Catherine B. Dick, "Bond Family of Tongue Creek," in Tales and Trials, *Tales and Trials*, 47.

11 "Bob Newbolt, Pioneer 1884," Newbolt fonds.

12 Loree, "My Sunset Childhood."

13 "Marjorie Linthicum," in Poirier, *Cowgirls*, 122–23.

14 Ibid.

15 Gretel Ehrlich, *The Solace of Open Spaces* (New York: Penguin, 1985), 14.

16 Springett, *For My Children's Children*, 106–7.

17 Inderwick, "A Lady and Her Ranch," 66.

18 O'Neil, "A Lady's Life on a Ranche," 506.

19 Ehrlich, *Solace of Open Spaces*, 5.

20 "Vernice Wearmouth," in Poirier et al., *A Voice of Her Own*, 9.

21 Carter, "Diversifying Ranching History," 156.

Appendix

1 Constance Loree, "My Sunset Childhood" (unpublished memoir, c.1970s), property of Loree family, Nanton, AB.

Bibliography

Primary Sources

Abbott, E. C. "Teddy Blue," and Helena Huntington Smith. *We Pointed Them North: Recollections of a Cowpuncher*. Norman: University of Oklahoma Press, 1939.

Banister, Amelia Brown. Fonds. M8364. Glenbow Archives, Calgary.

Baptie, Thomas and Gladys. Fonds. M2551. Glenbow Archives, Calgary.

Bartsch, Christian. Fonds. M62. Glenbow Archives, Calgary.

Bartsch, Grace. Fonds. M63 f.7. Glenbow Archives, Calgary.

Burton, Doris A. *Babe's Sunshine: I Made My Own*. Lethbridge, AB: Robins Southern Printing, 1990.

Calof, Rachel Bella. *Rachel Calof's Story: Jewish Homesteader on the Northern Plains*. Edited by J. Sanford Rikoon. Bloomington: Indiana University Press, 1995.

Census of Prairie Provinces, 1916: Population and Agriculture. Ottawa: 1918.

Cerney, Hazel, and Ethel Hunter. *The Silent Hills: The Kropinak Family of Chapel Rock*. Blairmore, AB: published by Hazel Cerney, 1992.

Cleaveland, Agnes Morley. *No Life for a Lady*. Boston: Houghton Mifflin, 1941.

Clifford, Ann. *Ann's Story: A Great Ranching Empire and the People Who Made It Work*. N.p.: Forever in Memory, 1995.

Cochrane, Billy and Evelyn. Fonds. M6552-1, M6552-2. Glenbow Archives, Calgary.

Cran, Mrs. George. *A Woman in Canada*. Toronto: Musson Book Company, 1910.

Dick, Catherine Bond. *Trails I've Ridden*. Calgary: Albertan Job Press, 1946.

Eggleston, Wilfrid. *Homestead on the Range*. Ottawa: Borealis, 1982.

Foothills Historical Society. *Chaps and Chinooks: A History West of Calgary*. Calgary: Foothills Historical Society, 1976.

Gardiner, Barbara. Fonds. M7283-72. Glenbow Archives, Calgary.

Gardiner, Claude. Fonds. M7283-49, M7283-50. Glenbow Archives, Calgary.

Gardiner, Claude. *Letters from an English Rancher*. Edited by Hugh Dempsey. Calgary: Glenbow Alberta Institute, 1988.

High River Pioneers' and Old Timers' Association. *Leaves from the Medicine Tree: A History of the Area Influenced by the Tree, and Biographies of Pioneers and Old Timers Who Came under Its Spell prior to 1900*. Altona, MB: Friesen, 1960.

Historical Committee of the Nightingale Community Association. *The English Colony: Nightingale and District*. Calgary: Macleod Printing & Mailing, 1979.

Hopkins, Monica. *Letters from a Lady Rancher*. Halifax: Formac, 1983.

Hugget, R. H., Fonds. M5792. Glenbow Archives, Calgary.

Inderwick, Ella. Fonds. M559, 1–26. Glenbow Archives, Calgary.

Inderwick, Mary E. "A Lady and Her Ranch." In *The Best from Alberta History*, edited by Hugh Dempsey, 65–77. Saskatoon: Western Producer Prairie Books, 1981.

Ings family documents, property of Loree family. Calgary Glenbow Archives.

Ings, Fredrick W. *Before the Fences: Tales from the Midway Ranch*. Calgary: McAra, 1980.

Kelly, L. V. *The Range Men: The Story of the Ranchers and Indians of Alberta*. 1913. Toronto: Coles, 1980.

LaGrandeur, Violet. "Memoirs of a Cowboy's Wife." 72-27/SE, 1–24. Provincial Archives of Alberta, Edmonton.

Lane, George and Elizabeth. Fonds. M652. Glenbow Archives, Calgary.

Long, Philip Sheridan (as told by T. B. Long). *Seventy Years a Cowboy*. Saskatoon: Freeman, 1965.

Loree, Constance. "My Sunset Childhood." Unpublished memoir, c.1970s. Property of Loree family, Nanton, AB.

Macleay, Maxine, and Dorothy Macleay. *The Rocking P Gazette*. 1923–25. Original issues, property of Clay Chattaway, Nanton, AB.

McEachran, Duncan. "A Journey over the Plains: From Fort Benton to Bow River and Back." Reprinted from *Montreal Gazette*, November 1881. Archives and Special Collections, University of Calgary.

Nanton and District Historical Society. *Mosquito Creek Roundup: Nanton-Parkland*. Calgary: Friesen, 1975.

Neil, Mrs. Catherine. Fonds. M4116. Glenbow Archives, Calgary.

Newbolt, Robert. "On Pine Creek." *Calgary Tribune*, 8 July 1887. Robert Newbolt Fonds. M2487. Glenbow Archives, Calgary.

Pincher Creek Historical Society. *"Prairie Grass to Mountain Pass": History of the Pioneers of Pincher Creek and District*. Calgary: Friesen, 1974.

Poirier, Thelma, ed. *Cowgirls: 100 Years of Writing the Range*. Red Deer, AB: Red Deer College Press, 1997.

Poirier, Thelma, Doris Bircham, JoAnn Jones-Hole, Anne Slade, and Susan A. Vogelaar, eds. *A Voice of Her Own*. Calgary: University of Calgary Press, 2005.

Randall, Isabel F. *A Lady's Ranch Life in Montana*. Edited by Richard L. Saunders. Norman: University of Oklahoma Press, 2004.

Roosevelt, Theodore. *Ranch Life and the Hunting-Trail*. Ann Arbor: University Microfilms, 1966.

Sivell, Rhoda. *Voices from the Range*. Toronto: T. Eaton Co., 1911.

Springett, Evelyn C. *For My Children's Children*. Montreal: Unity Press, 1937.

Stavely Historical Book Society. *The Butte Stands Guard: Stavely and District*. Calgary: Friesen, 1976.

Stewart, Elinore Pruitt. *Letters of a Woman Homesteader (1914)*. Boston: Houghton Mifflin, 1988.

St. Maur, Susan Margaret McKinnon. *Impressions of a Tenderfoot*. London: John Murray, 1890.

Stockmen's Memorial Foundation "Heritage Voices" Project, c.1980s. Bert Sheppard Library and Archives, Cochrane, AB.

Tales and Trials History Book Society. *Tales and Trials: A History of Longview and Surrounding Area*. Calgary: Northwest Printing & Lithography, 1977.

Thomson, Georgina H. *Crocus and Meadowlark Country: A Story of an Alberta Family.* Edmonton: Institute of Applied Art, 1963.

Zarn, George. *Above the Forks*. High River, AB: published by author, 1978.

Secondary Sources

Armitage, Susan H., and Elizabeth Jameson, eds. *The Women's West*. Norman: University of Oklahoma, 1987.

Bennett, John W. *Northern Plainsmen: Adaptive Strategy and Agrarian Life.* Chicago: Aldine, 1969.

Brado, Edward. *Cattle Kingdom: Early Ranching in Alberta*. Surrey, BC: Heritage House, 2004.

Breen, David H. *The Canadian Prairie West and the Ranching Frontier, 1874–1924*. Toronto: University of Toronto Press, 1983.

Carter, Sarah. "'He Country in Pants' No Longer: Diversifying Ranching History." In *Cowboys, Ranchers and the Cattle Business: Cross Border Perspectives on Ranching History*, edited by Sarah Carter, Simon Evans, and Bill Yeo, 155–66. Calgary: University of Calgary Press, 1997.

Cavanaugh, Catherine A. "The Limitations of the Pioneering Partnership: The Alberta Campaign for Homestead Dower, 1909–1925." *Canadian Historical Review* 74, no. 2 (1993): 198–225. https://doi.org/10.3138/CHR-074-02-02.

Cavanaugh, Catherine A. "No Place for a Woman: Engendering Western Canadian Settlement." *Western Historical Quarterly* 28, no. 4 (1997): 493–518. https://doi.org/10.2307/969883.

Clayton, Lawrence. "Today's Cowboy: Coping with a Myth." In *The Cowboy Way: An Exploration of History and Culture*, edited by Paul H. Carlson, 201–8. Lubbock: Texas Tech University Press, 2000.

Dempsey, Hugh A. *The Golden Age of the Canadian Cowboy.* Calgary: Fifth House, 1995.

Dunae, Patrick. *Gentlemen Emigrants: From the British Public Schools to the Canadian Frontier.* Vancouver: Douglas & McIntyre, 1981.

Ehrlich, Gretel. *The Solace of Open Spaces.* New York: Penguin, 1985.

Elofson, Warren M. *Cowboys, Gentlemen, and Cattle Thieves: Ranching on the Western Frontier.* Montreal and Kingston: McGill-Queen's University Press, 2000.

Elofson, Warren M. *Frontier Cattle Ranching in the Land and Times of Charlie Russell*. Montreal and Kingston: McGill-Queen's University Press, 2004.

Elofson, Warren M. "Not Just a Cowboy: The Practice of Ranching in Southern Alberta, 1881–1914." *Canadian Papers in Rural History* 10 (1996): 205–16.

Elofson, Warren M. *Somebody Else's Money: The Walrond Ranch Story, 1883–1907*. Calgary: University of Calgary Press, 2009.

Evans, Simon. *The Bar U and Canadian Ranching History*. Calgary: University of Calgary Press, 2009.

Evans, Simon. *Prince Charming Goes West: The Story of the E.P. Ranch*. Calgary: University of Calgary Press, 1993.

Ewing, Sherm. *The Range*. Missoula, MT: Mountain Press Publishing, 1990.

Fairbanks, Carol, and Sara Brooks Sundberg. "Farm Women on the Canadian Prairie Frontier: The Helpmate Image." In *Farm Women on the Prairie Frontier: A Sourcebook for Canada and the United States*, 71–90. Metuchen, NJ: Scarecrow, 1983.

Ference, Ermeline Ann. "Literature associated with Ranching in Southern Alberta." Master's thesis, University of Alberta, 1971.

Flood, Elizabeth Clair. *Cowgirls: Women of the Wild West*. Santa Fe: Zon International, 2000.

Flood, Elizabeth Clair, and William Manns. *Cowgirls: Women of the Wild West (Postcards)*. Santa Fe: Zon International, 2003.

Foran, Max. *Trails and Trials: Markets and Land Use in Alberta Beef Cattle Industry, 1881–1948*. Calgary: University of Calgary Press, 2003.

Garceau, Dee. "Single Women Homesteaders and the Meanings of Independence: Places on the Map, Places in the Mind." *Frontiers: A Journal of Women Studies* 15, no. 3 (1995): 1–26. https://doi.org/10.2307/3346783.

Handy-Marchello, Barbara. *Women of the Northern Plains: Gender and Settlement on the Frontier Homestead, 1870–1930*. St. Paul: Minnesota Historical Society Press, 2005.

Horne, Robert M. "James Fergus: Frontier Businessman, Miner, Rancher, Free Thinker." PhD diss., University of Montana, 1971.

Hussa, Linda. *The Family Ranch: Land, Children, and Tradition in the American West*. Reno: University of Nevada Press, 2009.

Jameson, Elizabeth. "Connecting the Women's Wests." In *One Step over the Line: Toward a History of Women in the North American Wests*, edited by Elizabeth Jameson and Sheila McManus, 5–28. Edmonton: University of Alberta Press, 2008.

Jameson, Sheilagh S. "Women in the Southern Alberta Ranch Community, 1881–1914." In *The Canadian West: Social Change and Economic Development*, edited by Henry C. Klassen, 63–78. Calgary: University of Calgary, Comprint Publishing, 1977.

Jensen, Joan M. *With These Hands: Women Working on the Land*. Old Westbury, NY: Feminist Press, 1981.

Jordan, Teresa. *Cowgirls: Women of the American West*. 2nd ed. Lincoln: University of Nebraska Press, 1992.

Jordan, Teresa. *North American Cattle-Ranching Frontiers: Origins, Diffusion, Differentiation*. Albuquerque: University of New Mexico Press, 1993.

Kay, Jeanne. "Landscapes of Women and Men: Rethinking the Regional Historical Geography of United States and Canada." *Journal of Historical Geography* 17, no. 4 (1991): 435–52. https://doi.org/10.1016/0305-7488(91)90026-R.

Kinnear, Mary. "'Do You Want Your Daughter to Marry a Farmer?': Women's Work on the Farm, 1922." In *Canadian Papers in Rural History*, vol. 5., edited by Donald H. Akenson, 137–53. Gananoque, ON: Langdale, 1988.

Kinnear, Mary. *A Female Economy: Women's Work in a Prairie Province, 1870–1970*. Montreal and Kingston: McGill-Queen's University Press, 1998.

Klassen, Henry C. "A Century of Ranching at the Rocking P and Bar S." In *Cowboys, Ranchers and the Cattle Business: Cross Border Perspectives on Ranching History*, edited by Sarah Carter, Simon Evans, and Bill Yeo, 101–22. Calgary: University of Calgary Press, 1997.

Klassen, Henry C. *Eye on the Future: Business People in Calgary and the Bow Valley, 1870–1900*. Calgary: University of Calgary Press, 2002.

Kozak, Nadine I. "Advice Ideals and Rural Prairie Realities: National and Prairie Scientific Motherhood Advice, 1920–29." In *Unsettled Pasts: Reconceiving the West through Women's History*, edited by Sarah Carter, Lesley Erickson, Patricia Roome, and Char Smith, 179–204. Calgary: University of Calgary Press, 2005.

Langford, Nanci. "Childbirth on the Canadian Prairies, 1880–1930." In *Telling Tales: Essays in Western Women's History*, edited by Catherine A.

Cavanaugh and Randi R. Warne. Vancouver: University of British Columbia Press, 2000.

Lounsberry, Lorain. "Wild West Shows and the Canadian West." In *Cowboys, Ranchers and the Cattle Business: Cross Border Perspectives on Ranching History*, edited by Sarah Carter, Simon Evans, and Bill Yeo, 139–52. Calgary: University of Calgary Press, 1997.

Maret, Elizabeth. *Women of the Range: Women's Roles in the Texas Beef Cattle Industry*. College Station: Texas A&M University Press, 1993.

Marriott, Alice. *Hell on Horses and Women*. Norman: University of Oklahoma Press, 1953.

McManus, Sheila. "Mapping the Alberta-Montana Borderlands: Race, Ethnicity and Gender in the Late Nineteenth Century." *Journal of American Ethnic History* 20, no. 3 (2001): 71–88.

Merrill, Karen M. "Whose Home on the Range?" *Western Historical Quarterly* 27, no. 4 (1996): 433–51. https://doi.org/10.2307/970532.

Millar, Nancy. *The Unmentionable History of the West*. Calgary: Red Deer Press, 2006.

Neth, Mary. *Preserving the Family Farm: Women, Community, and the Foundations of Agribusiness in the Midwest, 1900–1940*. Baltimore: Johns Hopkins University Press, 1995.

Pascoe, Peggy. "Western Women at the Cultural Crossroads." In *Trails: Toward a New Western History*, edited by Patricia Nelson Limerick, Clyde A. Milner, and Charles E. Rankin, 40–58. Lawrence: University Press of Kansas, 1991.

Potyondi, Barry. *In Palliser's Triangle: Living in the Grasslands, 1850–1930*. Saskatoon: Purich, 1995.

Prescott, Cynthia Culver. "'Why She Didn't Marry Him': Love, Power, and Marital Choice on the Far Western Frontier." *Western Historical Quarterly* 38, no. 1 (2007): 25–45. https://doi.org/10.1093/whq/38.1.25.

Rasmussen, Linda, Lorna Rasmussen, Candace Savage, and Anne Wheeler, eds. *A Harvest Yet to Reap: A History of Prairie Women*. Toronto: The Women's Press, 1976.

Riley, Glenda. *Women and Nature: Saving the "Wild" West*. Lincoln: University of Nebraska Press, 1999.

Savage, Candace. *Born to Be a Cowgirl: A Spirited Ride through the Old West*. Vancouver: Greystone, 2001.

Scott, Joan. "Gender: A Useful Category of Historical Analysis." *American Historical Review* 91, no. 5 (1986): 1053–75. https://doi.org/10.2307/1864376.

Scott, Joan. "Women's History." In *Gender and the Politics of History*, 15–27. New York: Columbia University Press, 1988.

Silverman, Eliane Leslau. *The Last Best West: Women on the Alberta Frontier, 1880 1930*. Calgary: Fifth House, 1998.

Slatta, R. W. *Comparing Cowboys and Frontiers*. Norman: University of Oklahoma Press, 1997.

Smith, Henry Nash. *Virgin Land: The American West as Symbol and Myth*. Cambridge, MA: Harvard University Press, 1950.

Strong-Boag, Veronica. "Pulling in Double Harness or Hauling a Double Load: Women, Work and Feminism on the Canadian Prairie." In *The Prairie West: Historical Readings*, 2nd ed., edited by R. Douglas Francis and Howard Palmer, 401–23. Edmonton: University of Alberta Press, 1992.

Thomas, Lewis G. *Ranchers' Legacy: Alberta Essays*. Edited by Patrick E. Dunae. Edmonton: University of Alberta Press, 1986.

Turner, Frederick Jackson. "The Significance of the Frontier in American History." In *Major Problems in the History of the American West: Documents and Essays*, edited by Clyde A. Milner, 2–21. Lexington, MA: Heath, 1989.

Van Cleve, Barbara. *Hard Twist: Western Ranch Women*. Santa Fe: Museum of New Mexico Press, 1995.

van Herk, Aritha. "Washtub Westerns." In *Unsettled Pasts: Reconceiving the West through Women's History*, edited by Sarah Carter, Lesley Erickson, Patricia Roome, and Char Smith, 251–66. Calgary: University of Calgary Press, 2005.

Voisey, Paul. *Vulcan: The Making of a Frontier Community*. Toronto: University of Toronto Press, 1988.

Webb, Walter P. *The Great Plains*. New York: Ginn & Company, 1931.

West, Elliott. "Families in the West." *OAH Magazine of History* 9, no. 1 (1994): 18–21. https://doi.org/10.1093/maghis/9.1.18.

West, Elliott. *Growing Up with the Country: Childhood on the Far Western Frontier*. Albuquerque: University of New Mexico Press, 1989.

Young, Nancy. "The Reins in Their Hands: Ranchwomen and the Horse in Southern Alberta 1880–1914." *Alberta History* 52, no. 1 (2004): 2–8.

Index

Page numbers in italics refer to images.

M

N

T

U

V

W

Y

Z